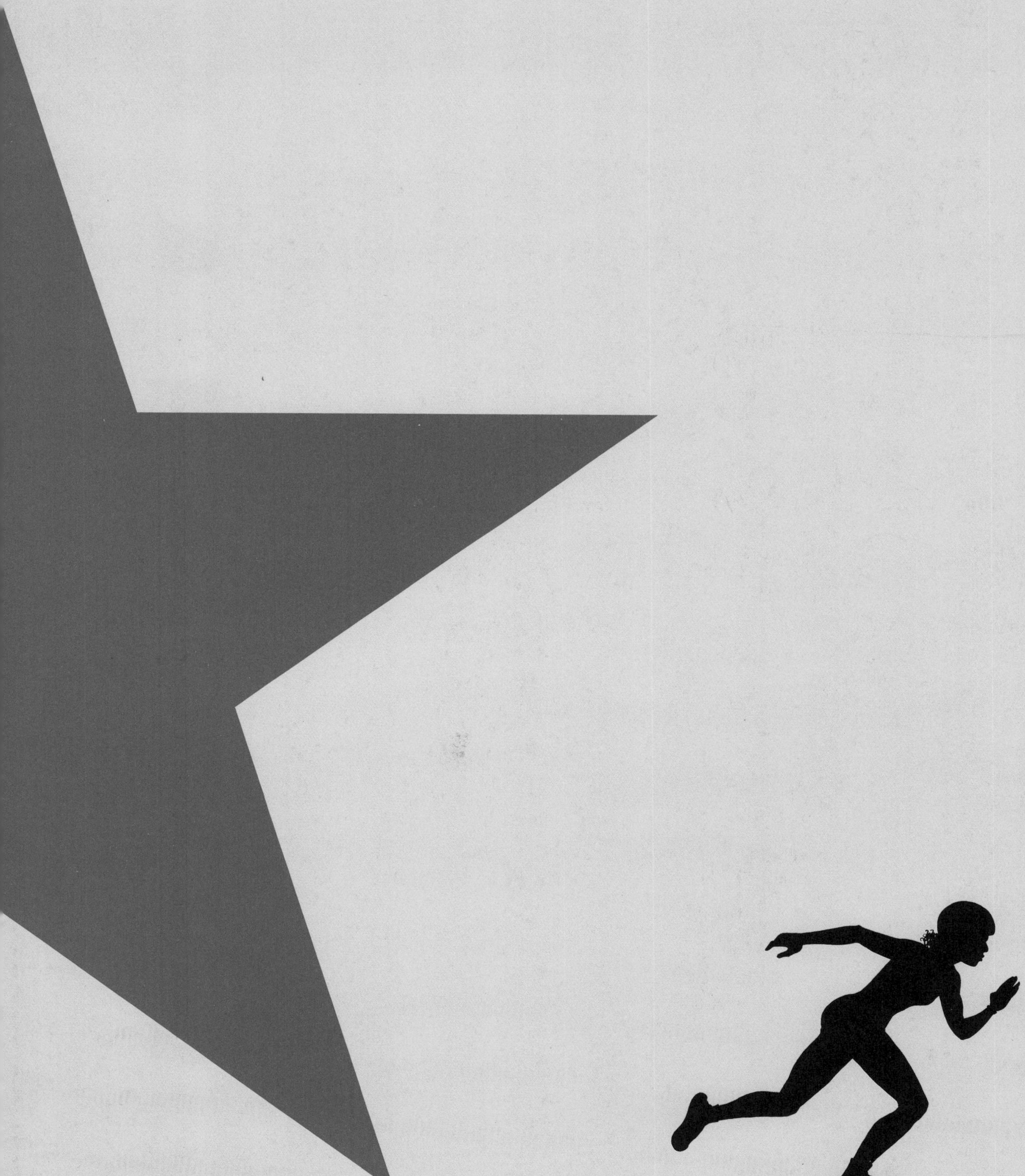

JESSICA ABEL
TRISH TRASH
ROLLERGIRL OF MARS

1
2
3

By Jessica Abel

Background and Design
Lydia Roberts

Colors
Walter

SUPER
GENIUS

New York

JESSICA ABEL
TRISH ① ② ③ TRASH
ROLLERGIRL OF MARS

Backgrounds and design by Lydia Roberts
Colors by Walter
Wikimarz.red art and colors by Lydia Roberts

Originally published in French as:
Trish Trash: Rollergirl sur Mars
Copyright © 2014 Jessica Abel and Dargaud.
All rights reserved.
www.dargaud.com
www.jessicaabel.com
All other editorial material © 2016 by Super Genius.

Super Genius books may be purchased for business or promotional use. For information on bulk purchases please contact Macmillan Corporate and Premium Sales Department at (800) 221-7945 x 5442

Super Genius graphic novels are also available digitally wherever e-books are sold.

Super Genius is an imprint of Papercutz.

Dawn Guzzo — Production
Brittanie Black — Production Coordinator
Jeff Whitman — Editor
Jim Salicrup
Editor-in-Chief

ISBN: 978-1-62991-614-9

Printed in China
November 2016

Distributed by Macmillan
First Super Genius Printing

Trish Trash has been a very, very long time coming. The list of people I am indebted to is extensive. I am thrilled to finally have the opportunity to acknowledge and thank everyone, even as I'm slightly paralyzed by fear that the tortured history of the book may mean that I've omitted someone.

Matt Madden, of course, is my ever-present one-man writer's room. I can't express how much I appreciate and love him for it. Thanks, too, to all my readers over the years: Benjamin Fisch, Kim Chaloner, JP Kim, Nancy Ethiel, Jeremy Sorese, Nick Bertozzi, and Jessica Hedrick.

For their invaluable help in the studio, my sincere thanks to Wyeth Yates, Li-Or Zaltzman, Hilary Allison, Eric Arroyo, Kou Chen, and Justine Sarlat.

To Bob Mecoy: for the first few years, this project was stranded in very muddy waters. Thank you for helping me to steer the course. To my editor, Thomas Ragon: without your unwavering interest in this project, I would never have picked up a pen. Thank you both.

The Dargaud creative team has brought this book to a level I've never even visited before. Thank you, Fanny Soubiran, Walter, Philippe Ravon, Renaud DeChateaubourg, Nicolas Thibaudin, and Eve Bardin. My thanks also go to my attentive production team at Super Genius, Jim Salicrup, Jeff Whitman, and Dawn Guzzo.

The early work of Alina Urusov, Sang Jun Ohn, and Ron Wimberly in thinking about and helping me imagine the visual world of Trish Trash was enormously helpful. Thank you.

For their expertise in roller derby and their generous help in clarifying my understanding of what the hell is going on out there, I want to thank Justine Sarlat, Zoë Michaels, Anaïs Ninja, and Molly Flogger.

And for their information and inspiration, I extend my deep thanks to Kim Stanley Robinson, NASA's Mars rover teams, Space X, Google Mars, MarsOne, and the Gotham Girls Roller Derby.

Finally, to my assistant Lydia Roberts—you've made this book so much more than I could have alone. Your imagination, intelligence, and determination are stamped on every page. Thank you for all you do.

For Aldara and Jasper. *Ad astra.*

-Jessica Abel

COMING SOON

TRISH TRASH # 1

TRISH TRASH # 2

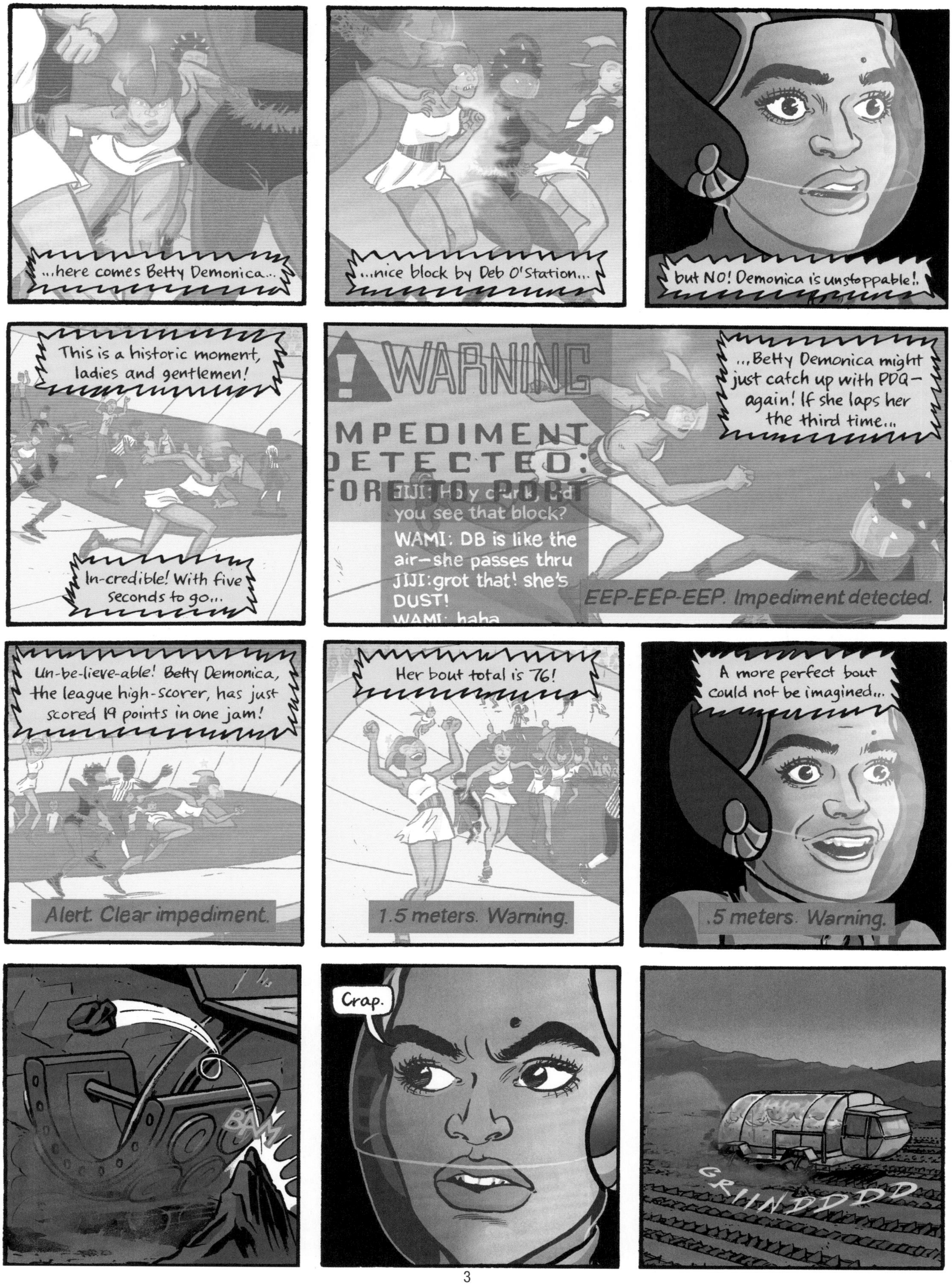
...here comes Betty Demonica...
...nice block by Deb O'Station...
but NO! Demonica is unstoppable!.
This is a historic moment, ladies and gentlemen!
In-credible! With five seconds to go...
WARNING
MPEDIMENT
ETECTED:
you see that block?
WAMI: DB is like the air—she passes thru
JIJI: grot that! she's DUST!
WAMI: haha
...Betty Demonica might just catch up with PDQ—again! If she laps her the third time...
EEP-EEP-EEP. Impediment detected.
Un-be-lieve-able! Betty Demonica, the league high-scorer, has just scored 19 points in one jam!
Alert. Clear impediment.
Her bout total is 76!
1.5 meters. Warning.
A more perfect bout could not be imagined...
.5 meters. Warning.
BAM
Crap.
GRIINDDDD

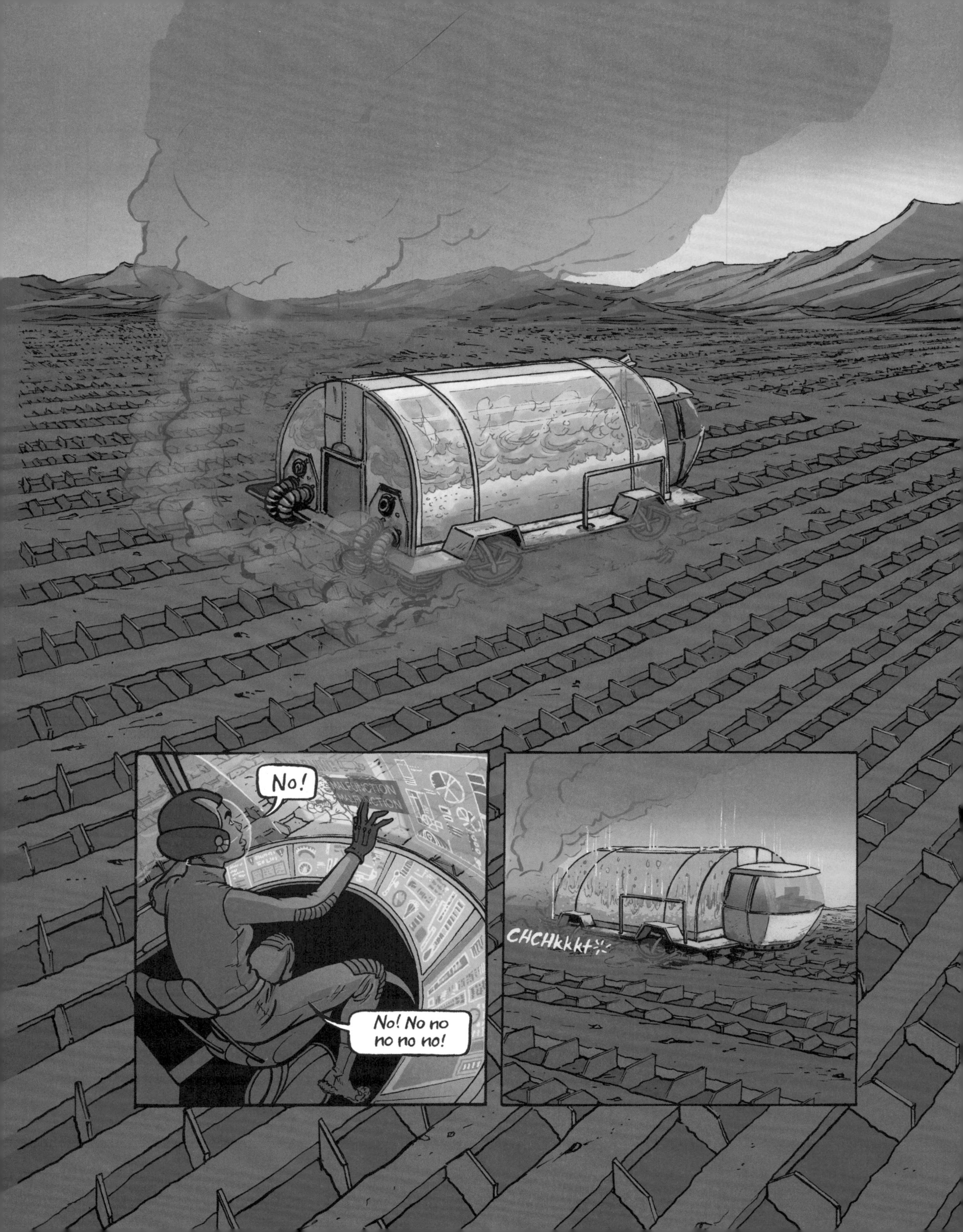
No!
MALFUNCTION
No! No no no no no!
CHCHkkkt

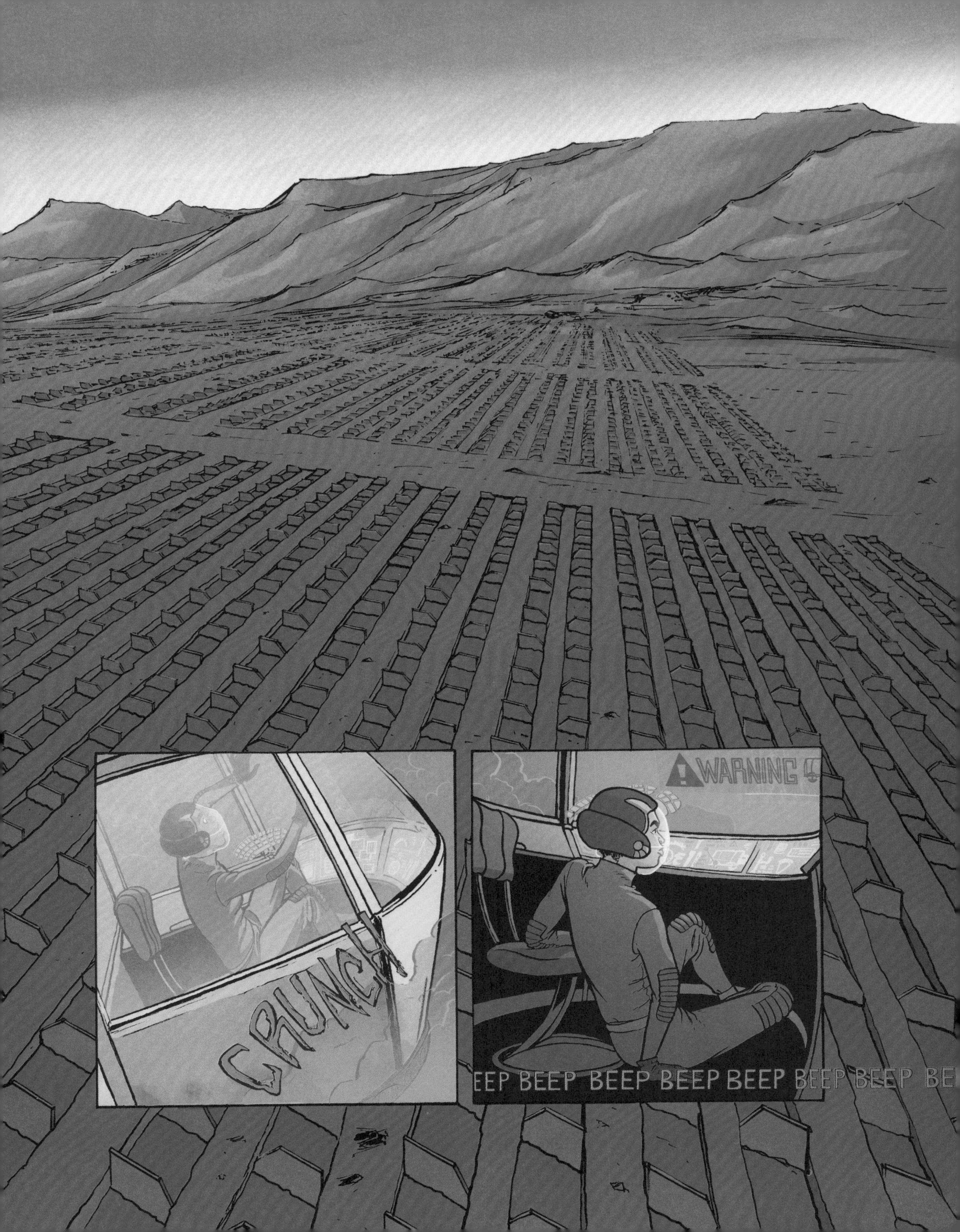
CRUNCH
WARNING
BEEP BEEP BEEP BEEP BEEP BEEP BEEP BEEP

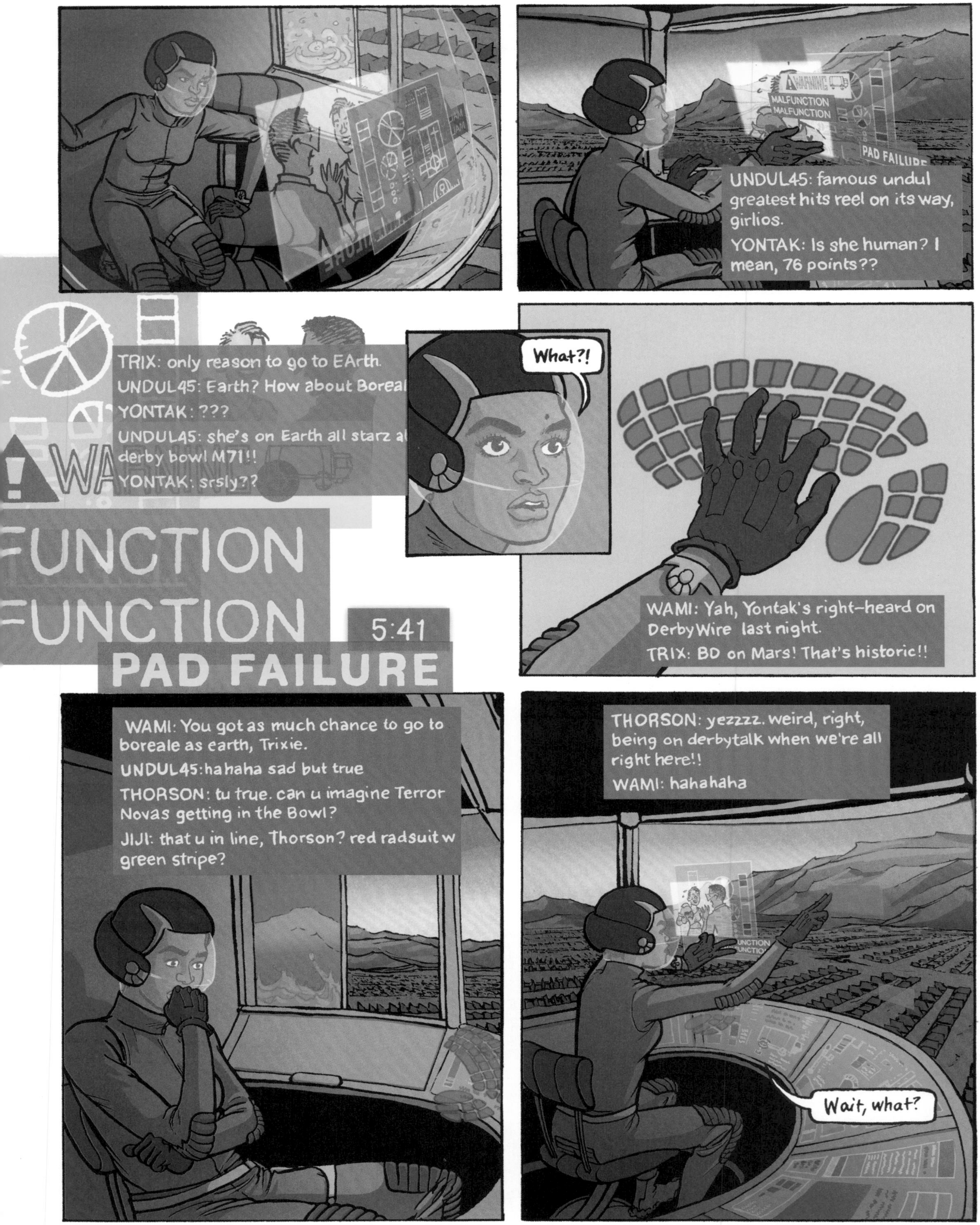
MALFUNCTION
MALFUNCTION
PAD FAILURE
UNDUL45: famous undul greatest hits reel on its way, girlios.
YONTAK: Is she human? I mean, 76 points??
TRIX: only reason to go to EArth.
UNDUL45: Earth? How about Boreal
YONTAK: ???
UNDUL45: she's on Earth all starz a
derby bowl M71!!
YONTAK: srsly??
FUNCTION
FUNCTION
5:41
PAD FAILURE
What?!
WAMI: Yah, Yontak's right—heard on DerbyWire last night.
TRIX: BD on Mars! That's historic!!
WAMI: You got as much chance to go to boreale as earth, Trixie.
UNDUL45: hahaha sad but true
THORSON: tu true. can u imagine Terror Novas getting in the Bowl?
JIJI: that u in line, Thorson? red radsuit w green stripe?
THORSON: yezzzz. weird, right, being on derbytalk when we're all right here!!
WAMI: hahahaha
Wait, what?

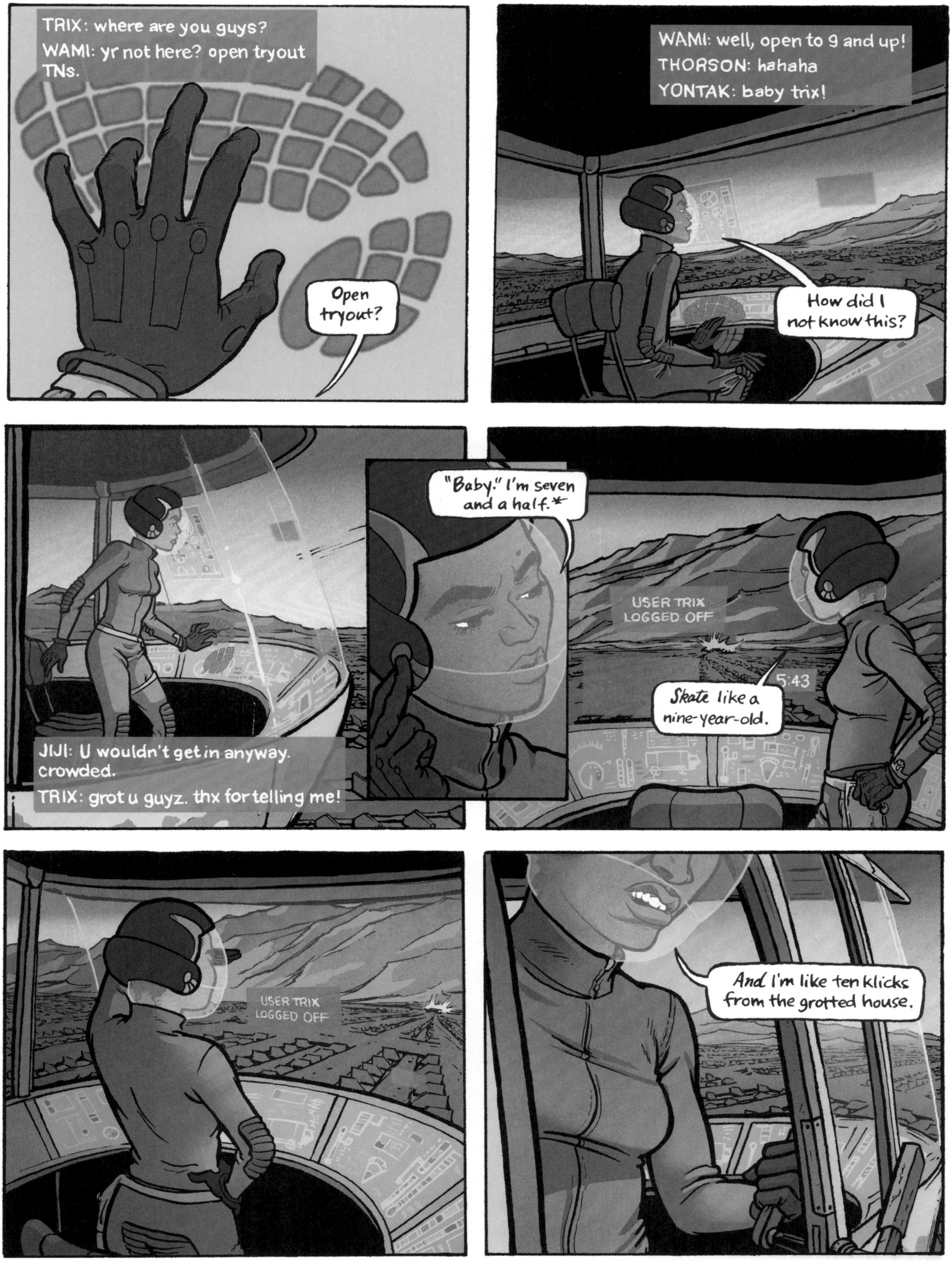
TRIX: where are you guys?
WAMI: yr not here? open tryout TNs.
Open tryout?
WAMI: well, open to 9 and up!
THORSON: hahaha
YONTAK: baby trix!
How did I not know this?
JIJI: U wouldn't get in anyway. crowded.
TRIX: grot u guyz. thx for telling me!
"Baby." I'm seven and a half.*
USER TRIX LOGGED OFF
5:43
Skate like a nine-year-old.
USER TRIX LOGGED OFF
And I'm like ten klicks from the grotted house.

*That's fifteen in Earth years. Martian years are twice as long as those on Earth.

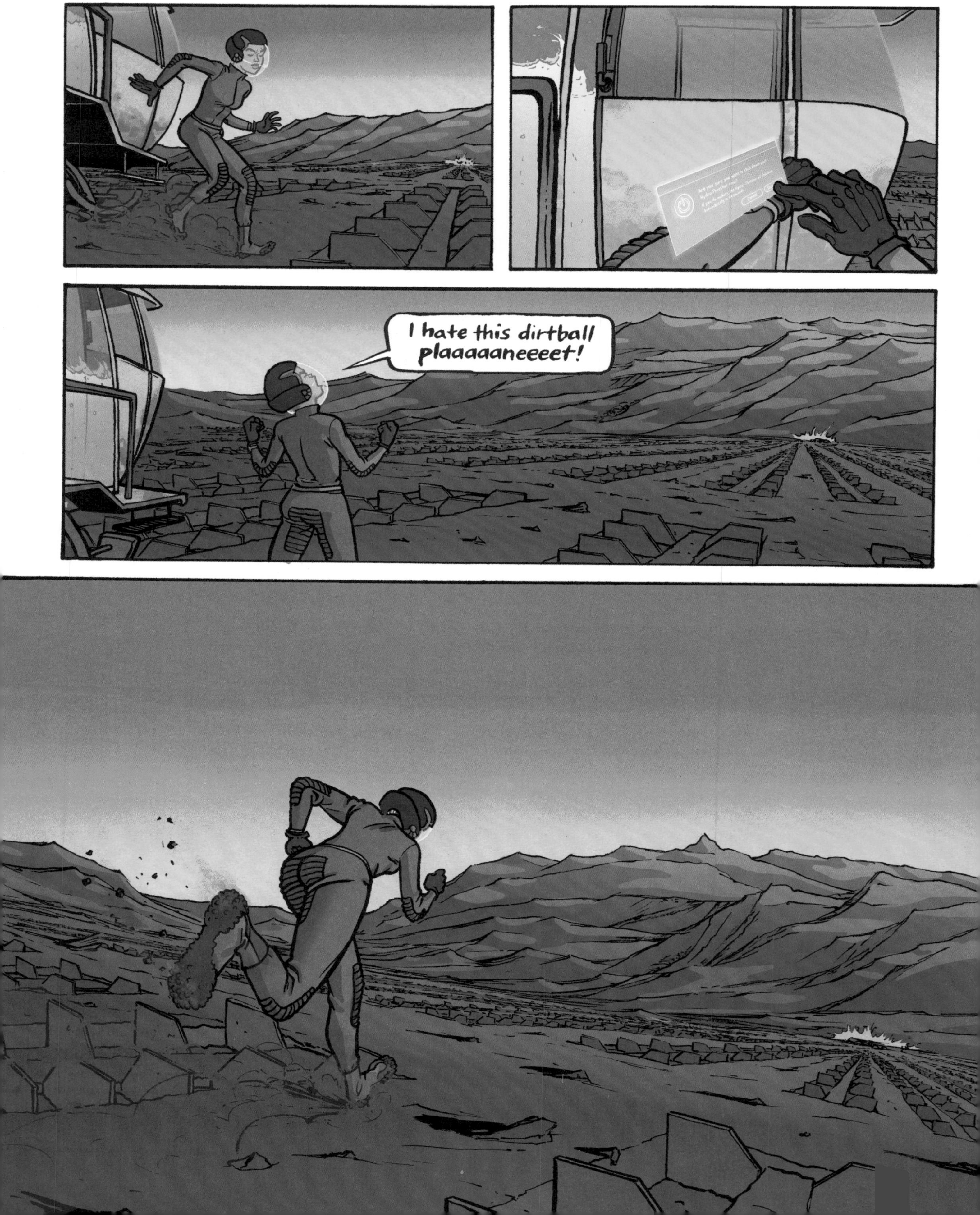
I hate this dirtball plaaaaaneeeet!

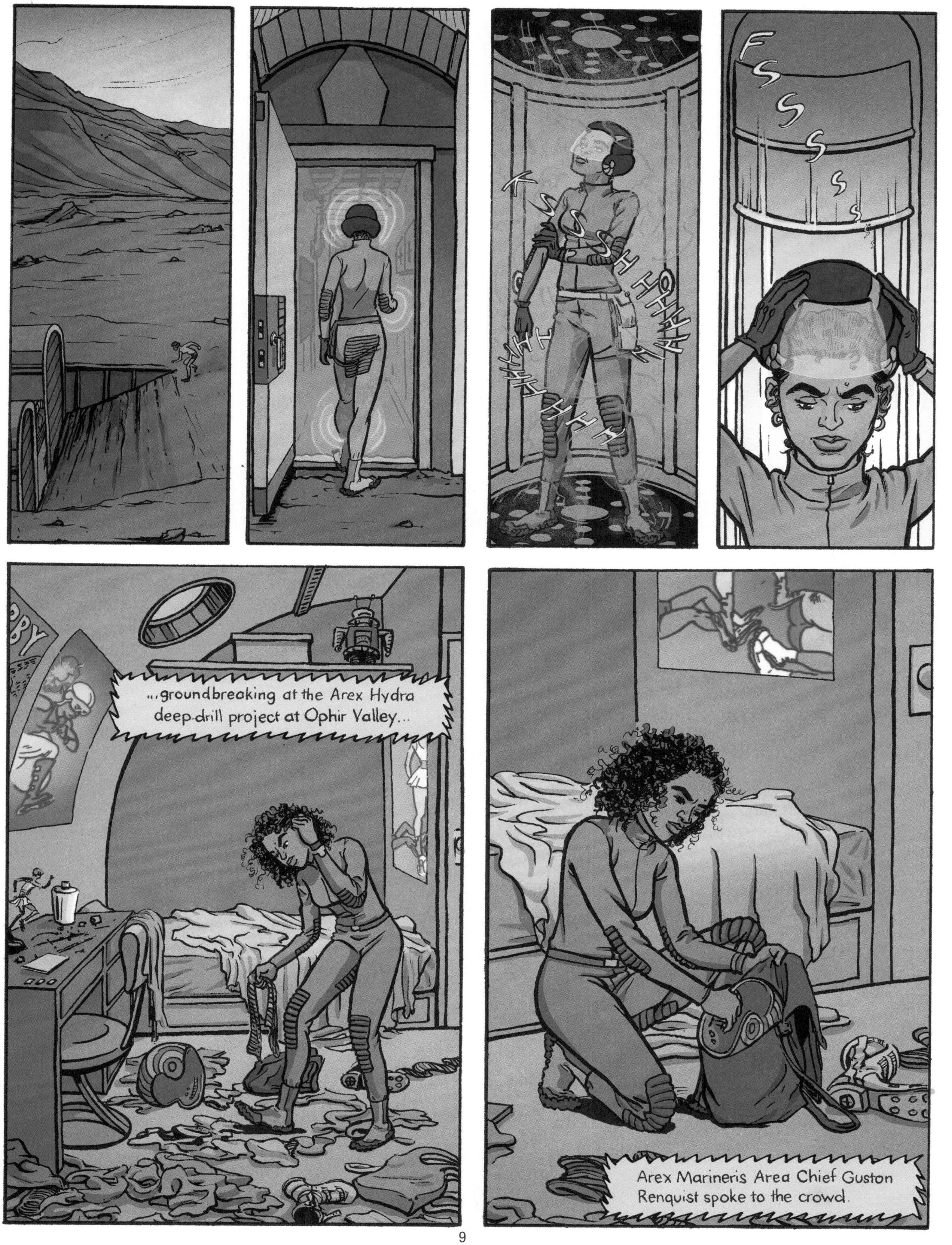
...groundbreaking at the Arex Hydra deep-drill project at Ophir Valley...
Arex Marineris Area Chief Guston Renquist spoke to the crowd.

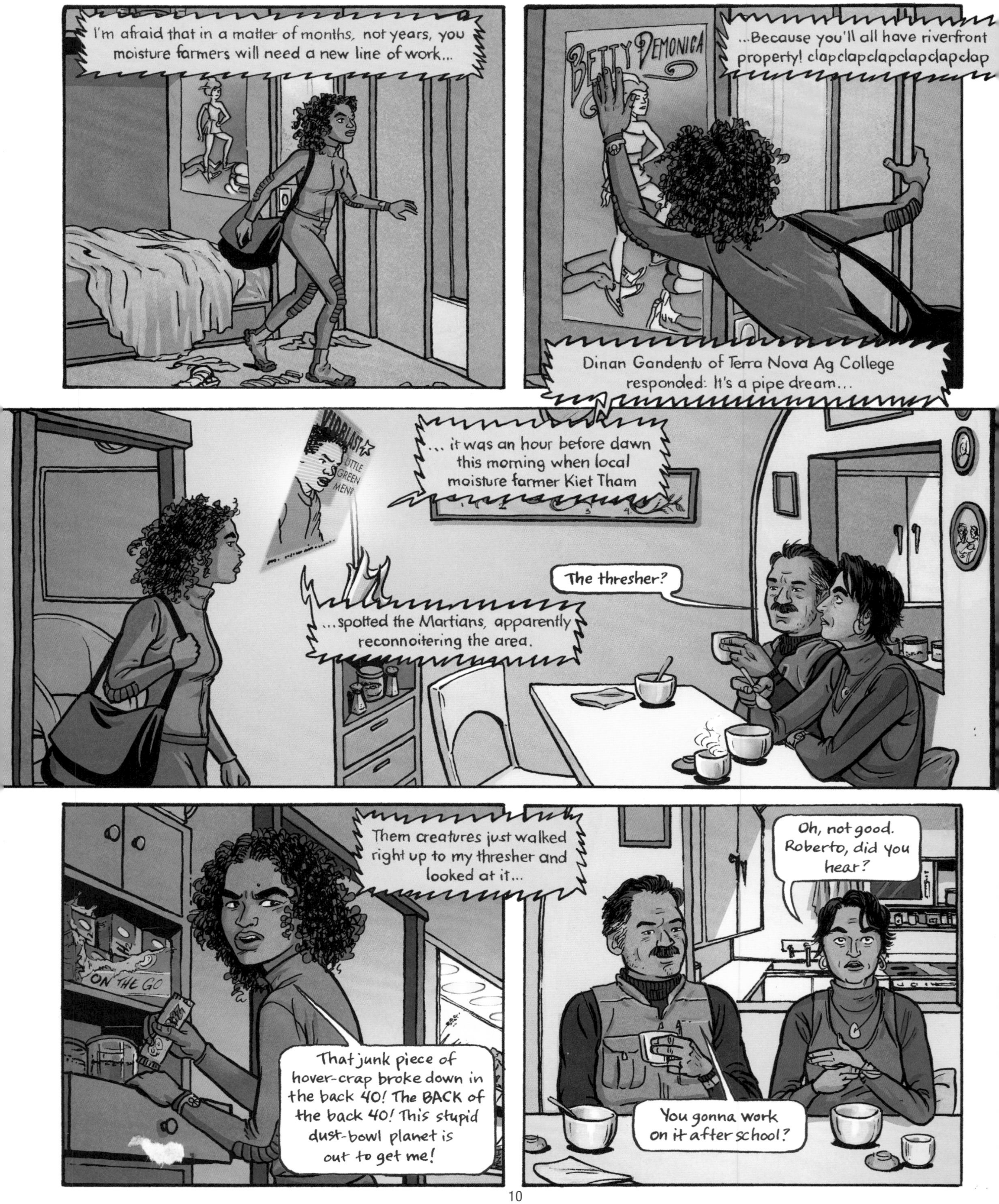
I'm afraid that in a matter of months, not years, you moisture farmers will need a new line of work...
BETTY DEMONICA
...Because you'll all have riverfront property! clapclapclapclapclapclap
Dinan Gandentu of Terra Nova Ag College responded: It's a pipe dream...
... it was an hour before dawn this morning when local moisture farmer Kiet Tham
...spotted the Martians, apparently reconnoitering the area.
LITTLE GREEN MEN?
The thresher?
Them creatures just walked right up to my thresher and looked at it...
ON THE GO
That junk piece of hover-crap broke down in the back 40! The BACK of the back 40! This stupid dust-bowl planet is out to get me!
Oh, not good. Roberto, did you hear?
You gonna work on it after school?

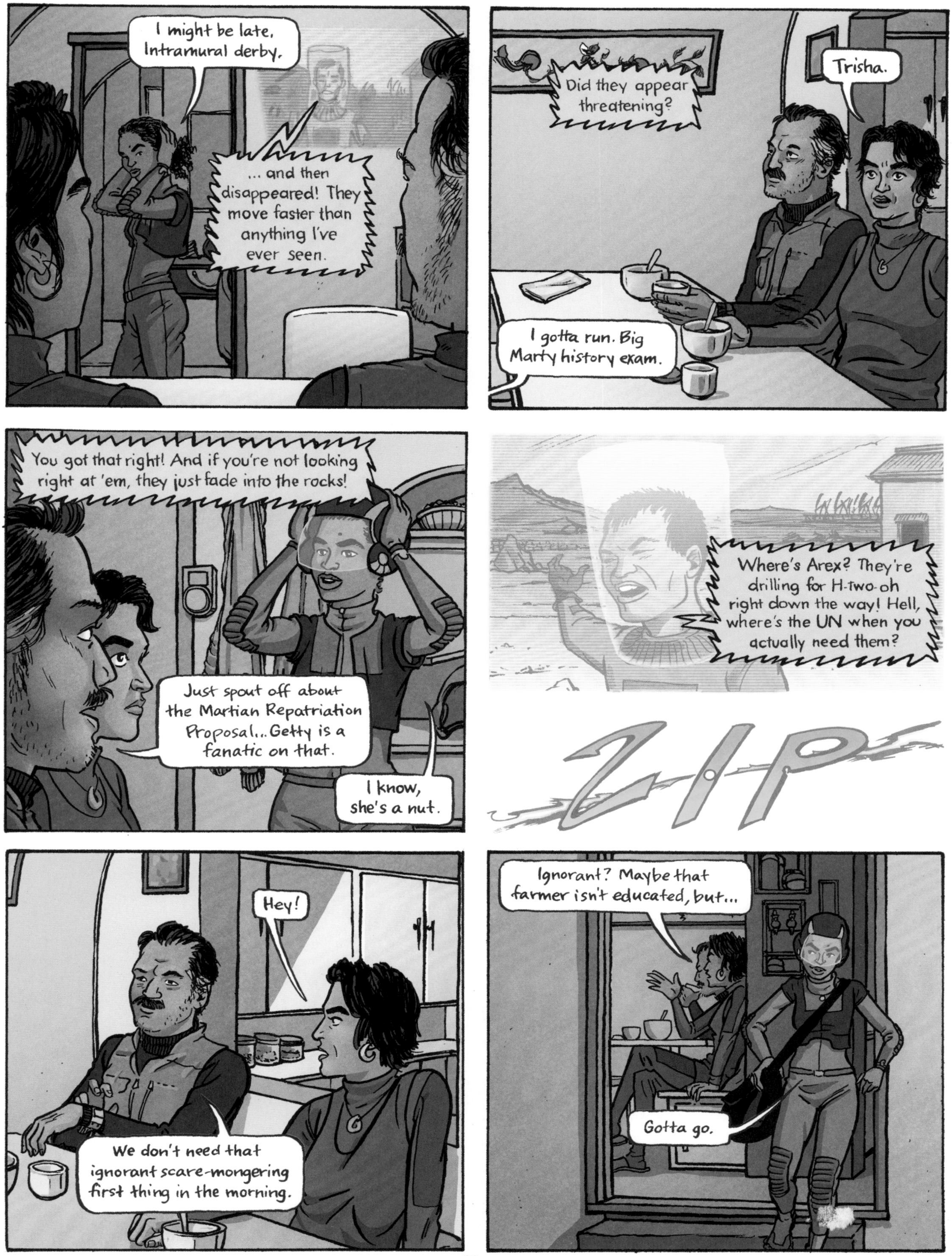
I might be late. Intramural derby.
... and then disappeared! They move faster than anything I've ever seen.
Did they appear threatening?
Trisha.
I gotta run. Big Marty history exam.
You got that right! And if you're not looking right at 'em, they just fade into the rocks!
Just spout off about the Martian Repatriation Proposal... Getty is a fanatic on that.
I know, she's a nut.
Where's Arex? They're drilling for H-two-oh right down the way! Hell, where's the UN when you actually need them?
ZIP
Hey!
We don't need that ignorant scare-mongering first thing in the morning.
Ignorant? Maybe that farmer isn't educated, but...
Gotta go.

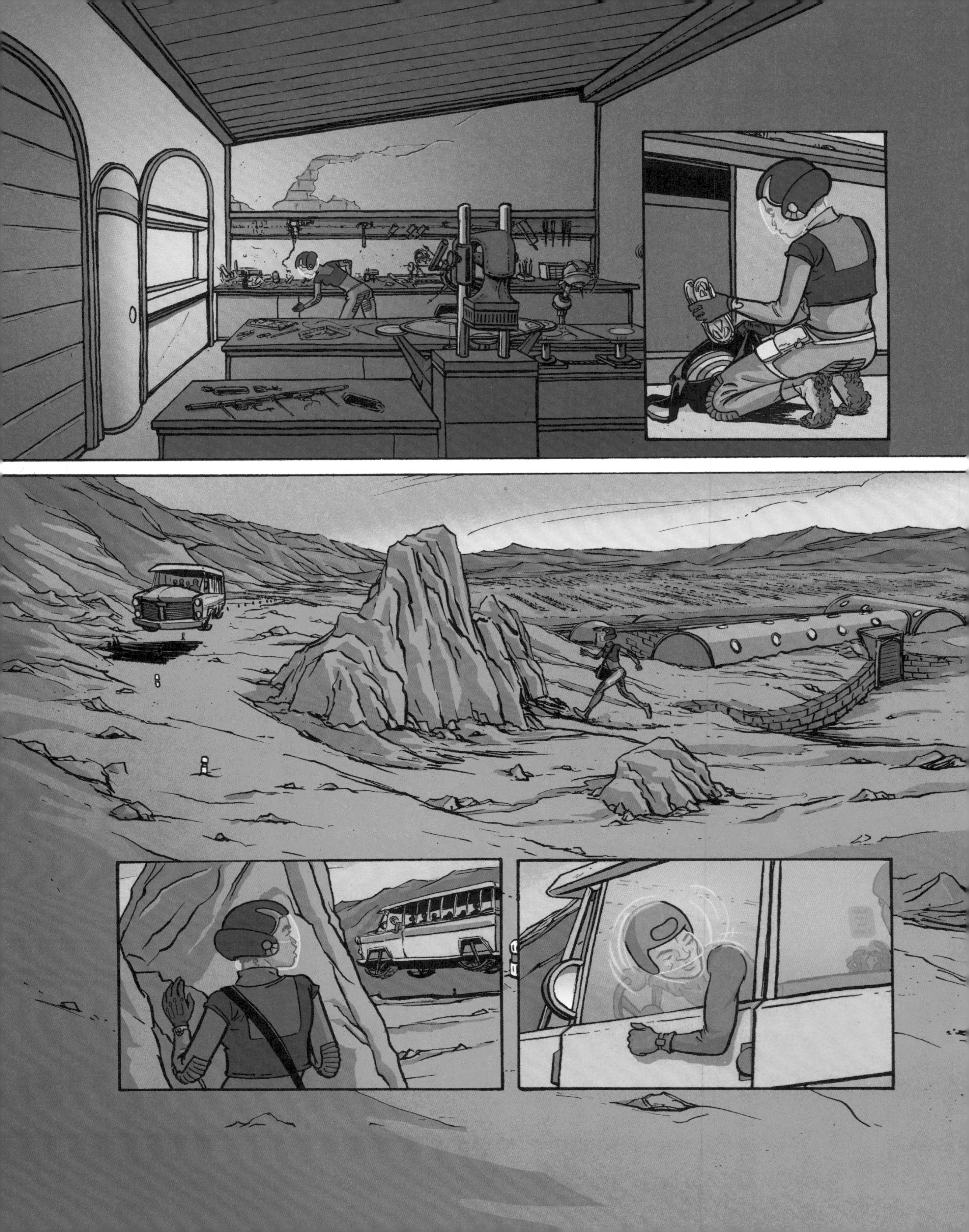

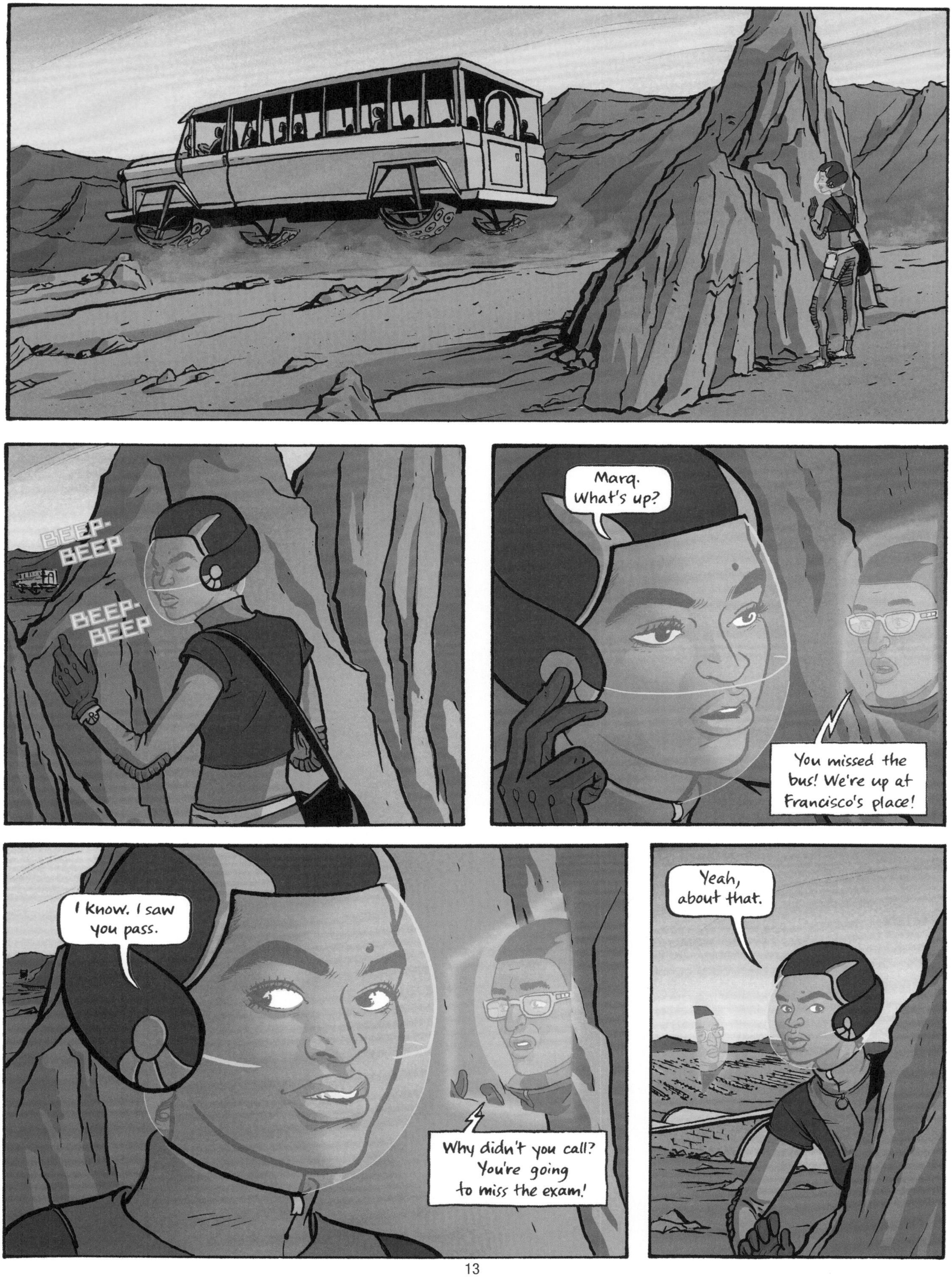
BEEP-BEEP
BEEP-BEEP
Marq. What's up?
You missed the bus! We're up at Francisco's place!
I know. I saw you pass.
Why didn't you call? You're going to miss the exam!
Yeah, about that.

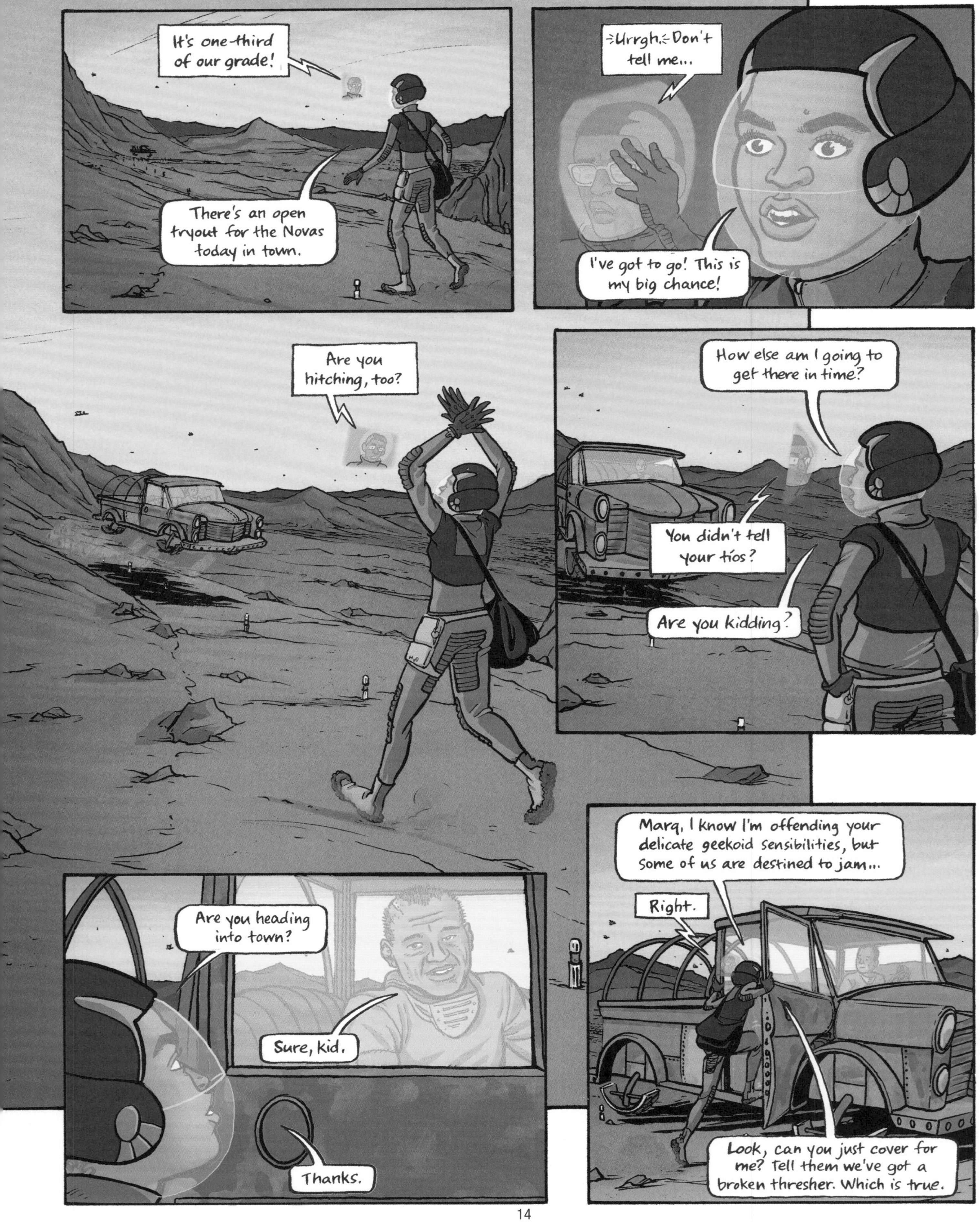
It's one-third of our grade!
There's an open tryout for the Novas today in town.
≈Urrgh.≈ Don't tell me...
I've got to go! This is my big chance!
Are you hitching, too?
How else am I going to get there in time?
You didn't tell your tíos?
Are you kidding?
Are you heading into town?
Sure, kid.
Thanks.
Marq, I know I'm offending your delicate geekoid sensibilities, but some of us are destined to jam...
Right.
Look, can you just cover for me? Tell them we've got a broken thresher. Which is true.

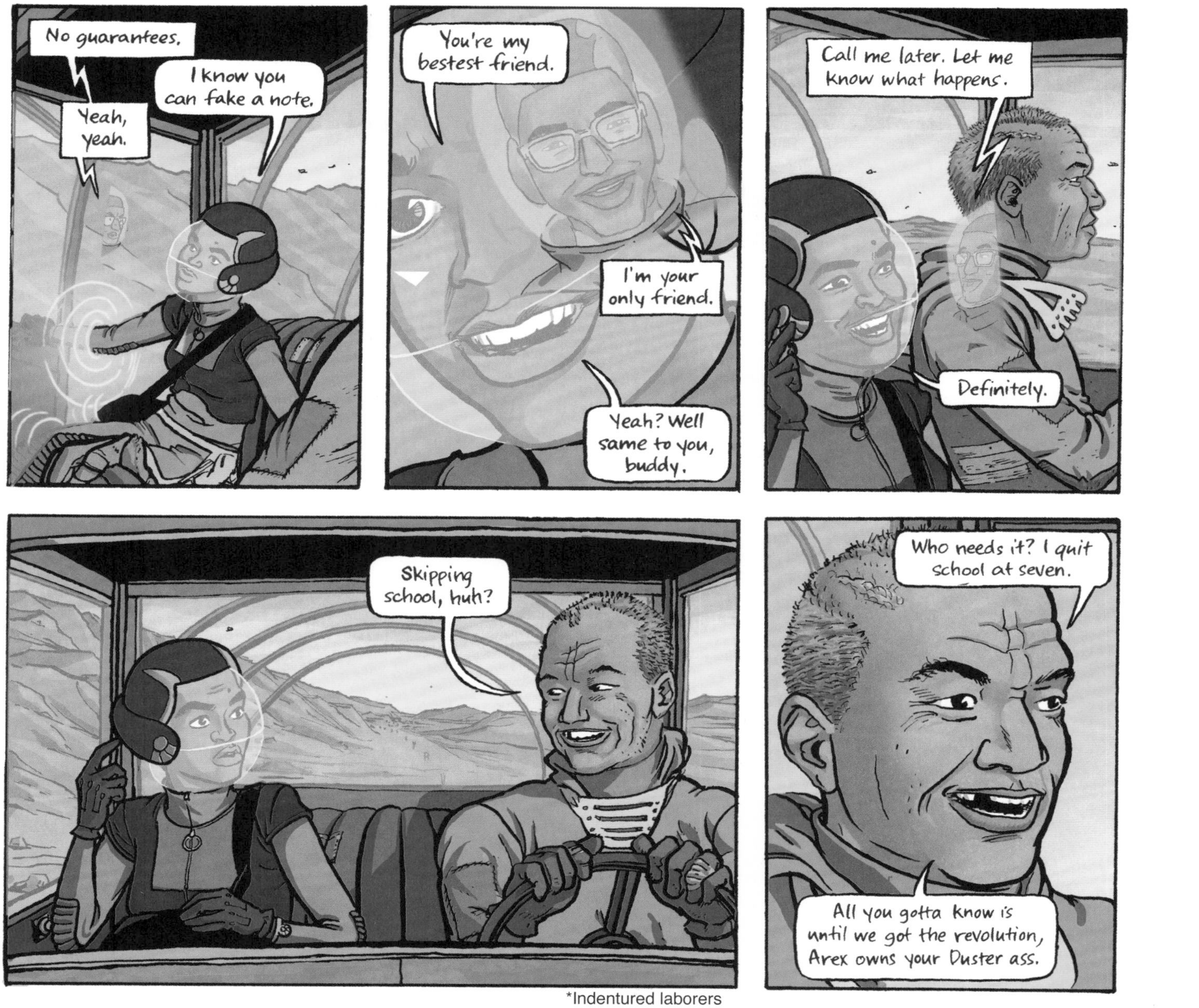
No guarantees.
I know you can fake a note.
Yeah, yeah.
You're my bestest friend.
I'm your only friend.
Yeah? Well same to you, buddy.
Call me later. Let me know what happens.
Definitely.
Skipping school, huh?
Who needs it? I quit school at seven.
All you gotta know is until we got the revolution, Arex owns your Duster ass.

*Indentured laborers

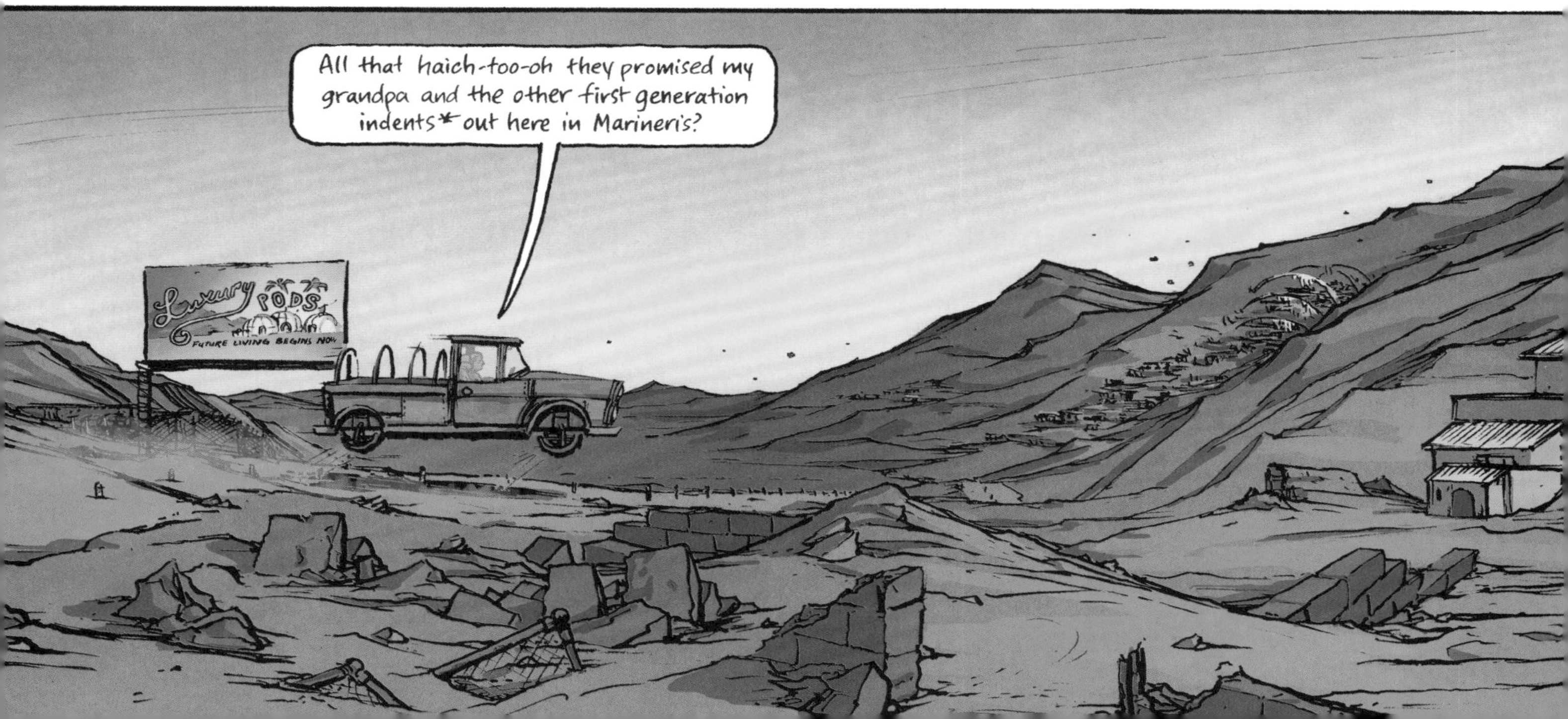
All that haich-too-oh they promised my grandpa and the other first generation indents* out here in Marineris?
Luxury PODS
FUTURE LIVING BEGINS NOW

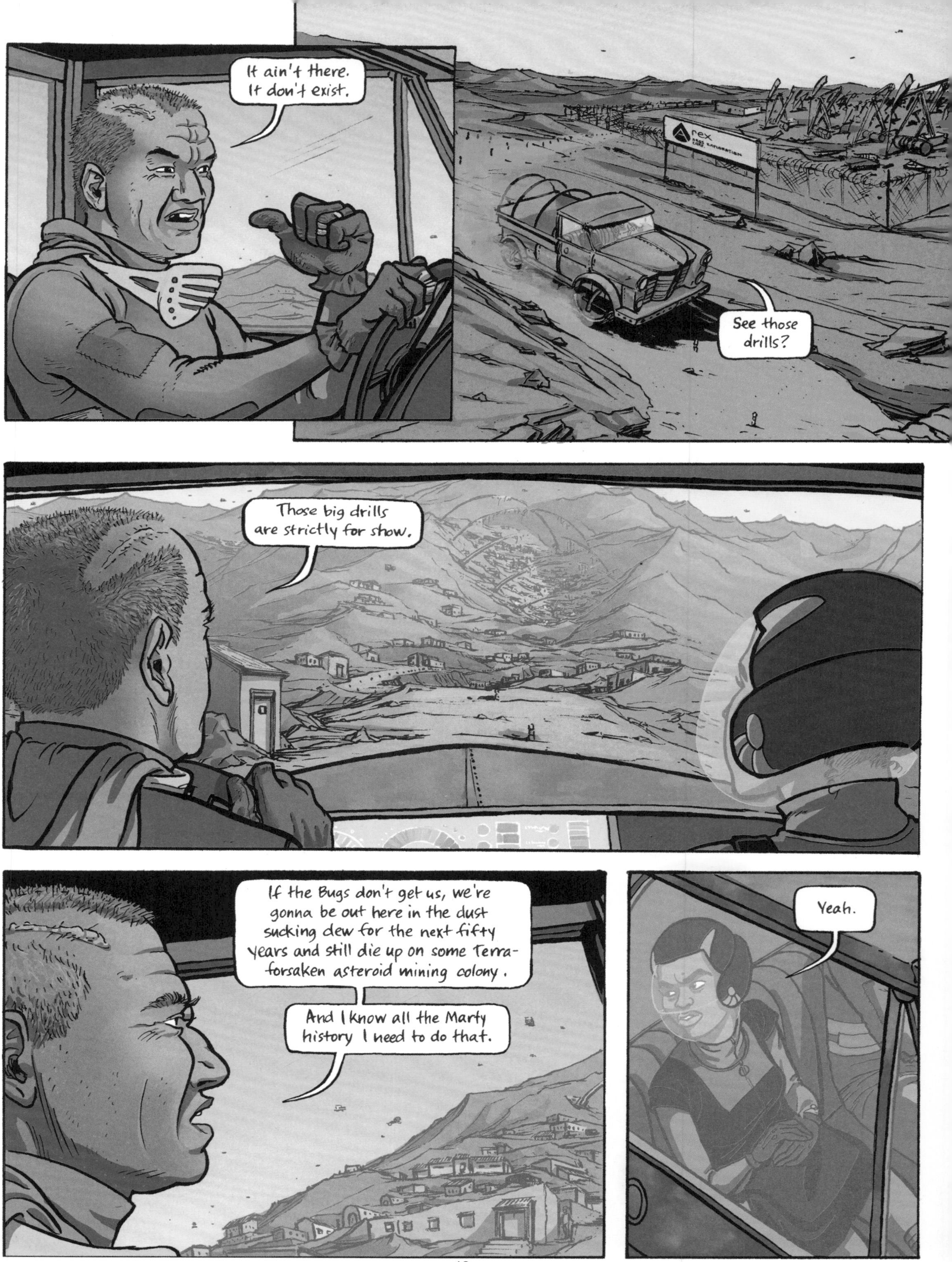
It ain't there. It don't exist.
See those drills?
Those big drills are strictly for show.
If the Bugs don't get us, we're gonna be out here in the dust sucking dew for the next fifty years and still die up on some Terra-forsaken asteroid mining colony.
And I know all the Marty history I need to do that.
Yeah.

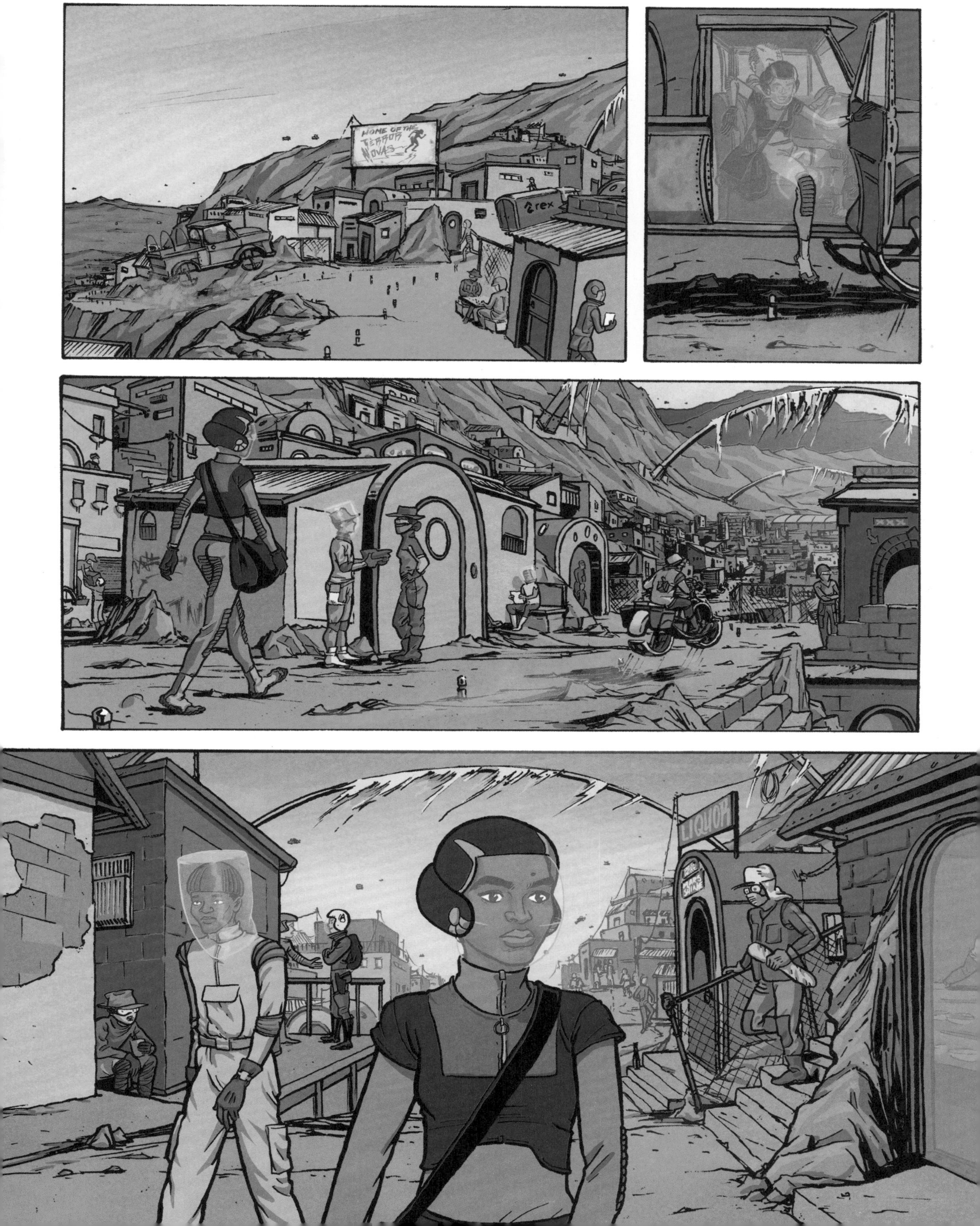
HOME OF THE TERROR NOVAS
rex
LIQUOR

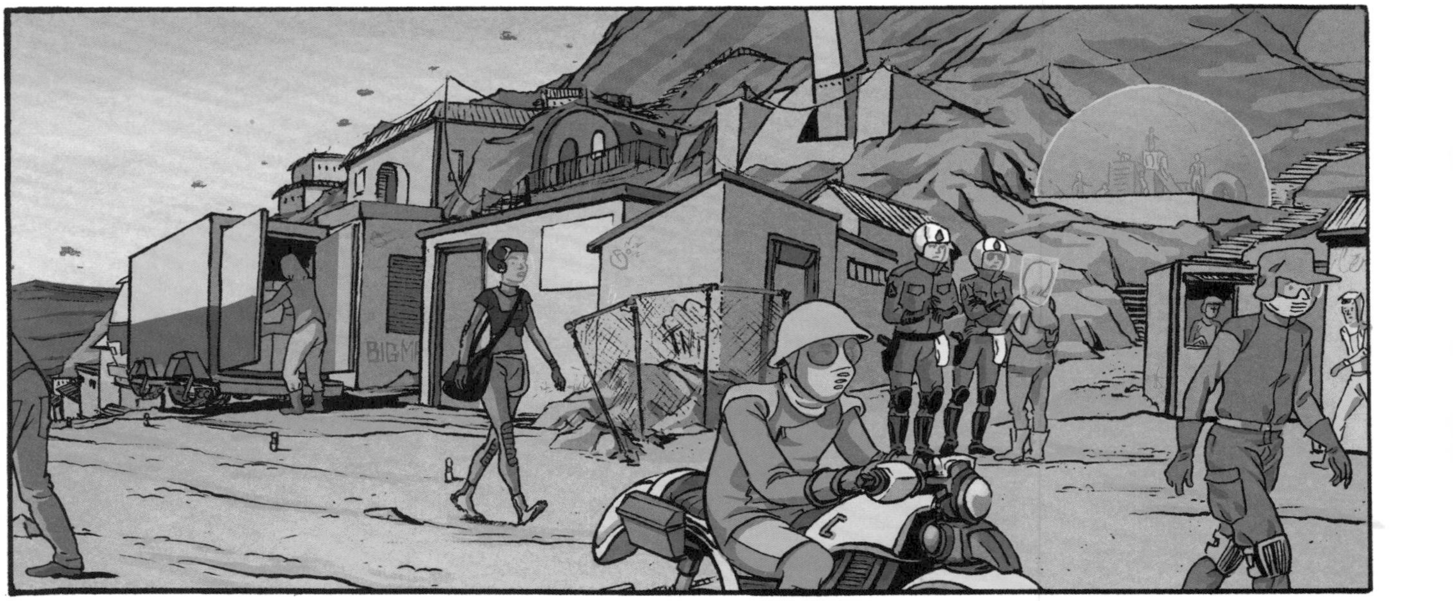
BIG M

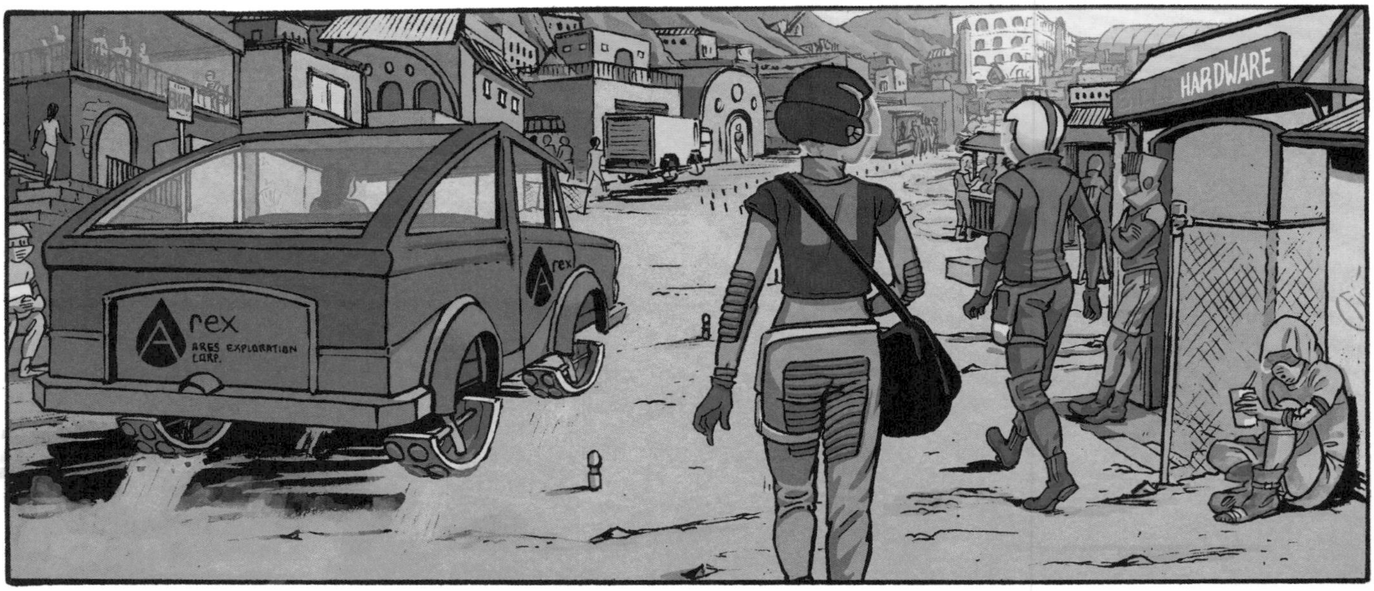
HARDWARE
rex
ARES EXPLORATION CORP.

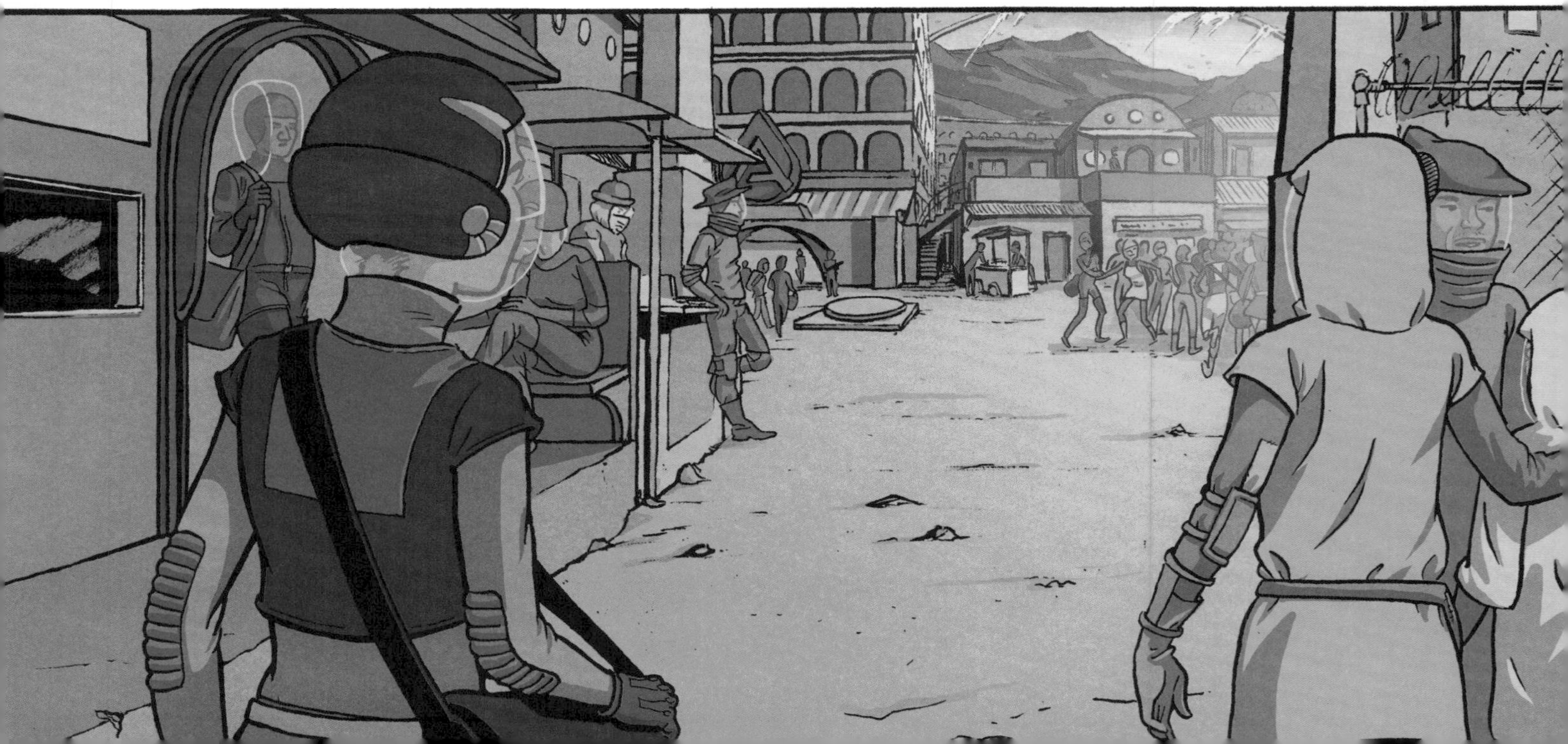

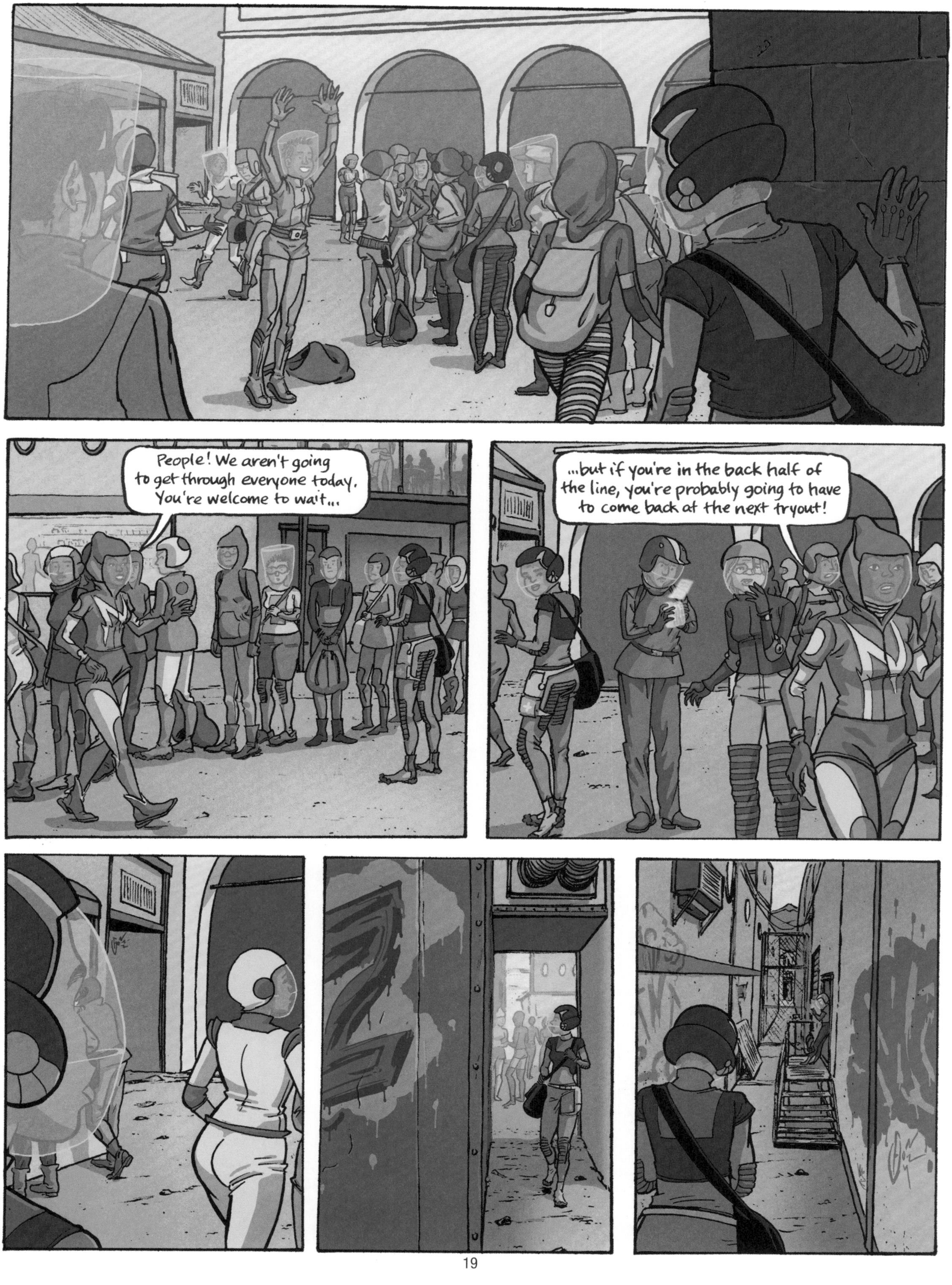
People! We aren't going to get through everyone today. You're welcome to wait...
...but if you're in the back half of the line, you're probably going to have to come back at the next tryout!

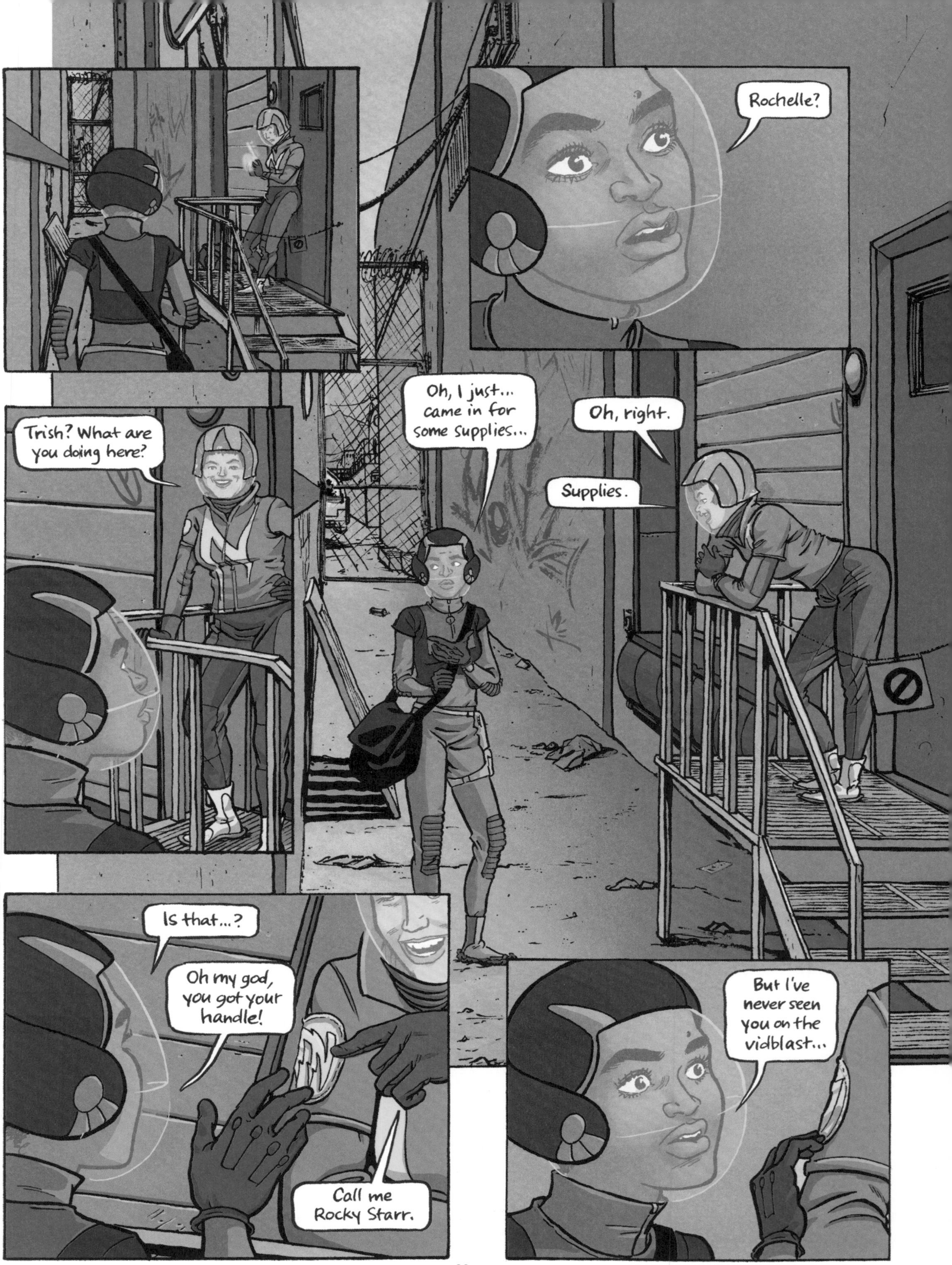
Rochelle?
Trish? What are you doing here?
Oh, I just... came in for some supplies...
Oh, right.
Supplies.
Is that...?
Oh my god, you got your handle!
Call me Rocky Starr.
But I've never seen you on the vidblast...

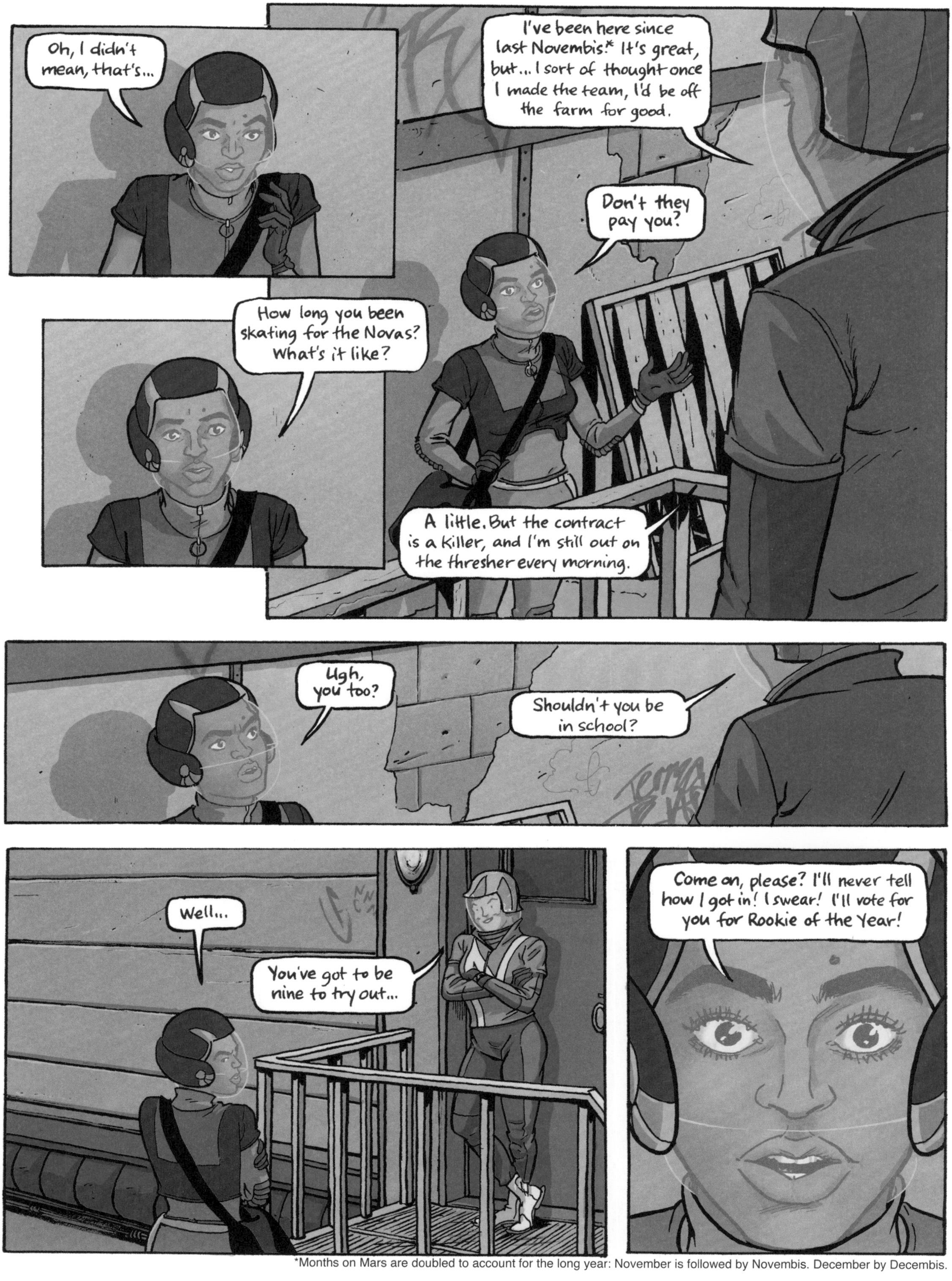
Oh, I didn't mean, that's...
I've been here since last Novembis.* It's great, but... I sort of thought once I made the team, I'd be off the farm for good.
How long you been skating for the Novas? What's it like?
Don't they pay you?
A little. But the contract is a killer, and I'm still out on the thresher every morning.
Ugh, you too?
Shouldn't you be in school?
Well...
You've got to be nine to try out...
Come on, please? I'll never tell how I got in! I swear! I'll vote for you for Rookie of the Year!

*Months on Mars are doubled to account for the long year: November is followed by Novembis. December by Decembis.

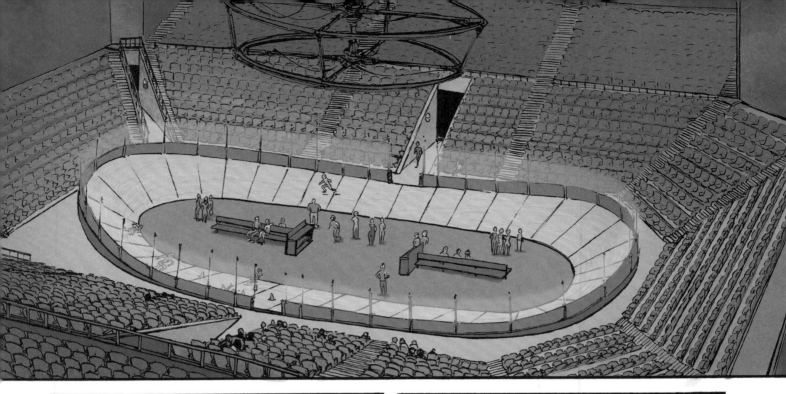

Look, there's Hanna Barbarian!

We're ready for the next group here—group four, get lined up!

OK, ladies, we're going to run a couple of drills to see what you can do.

Get set!

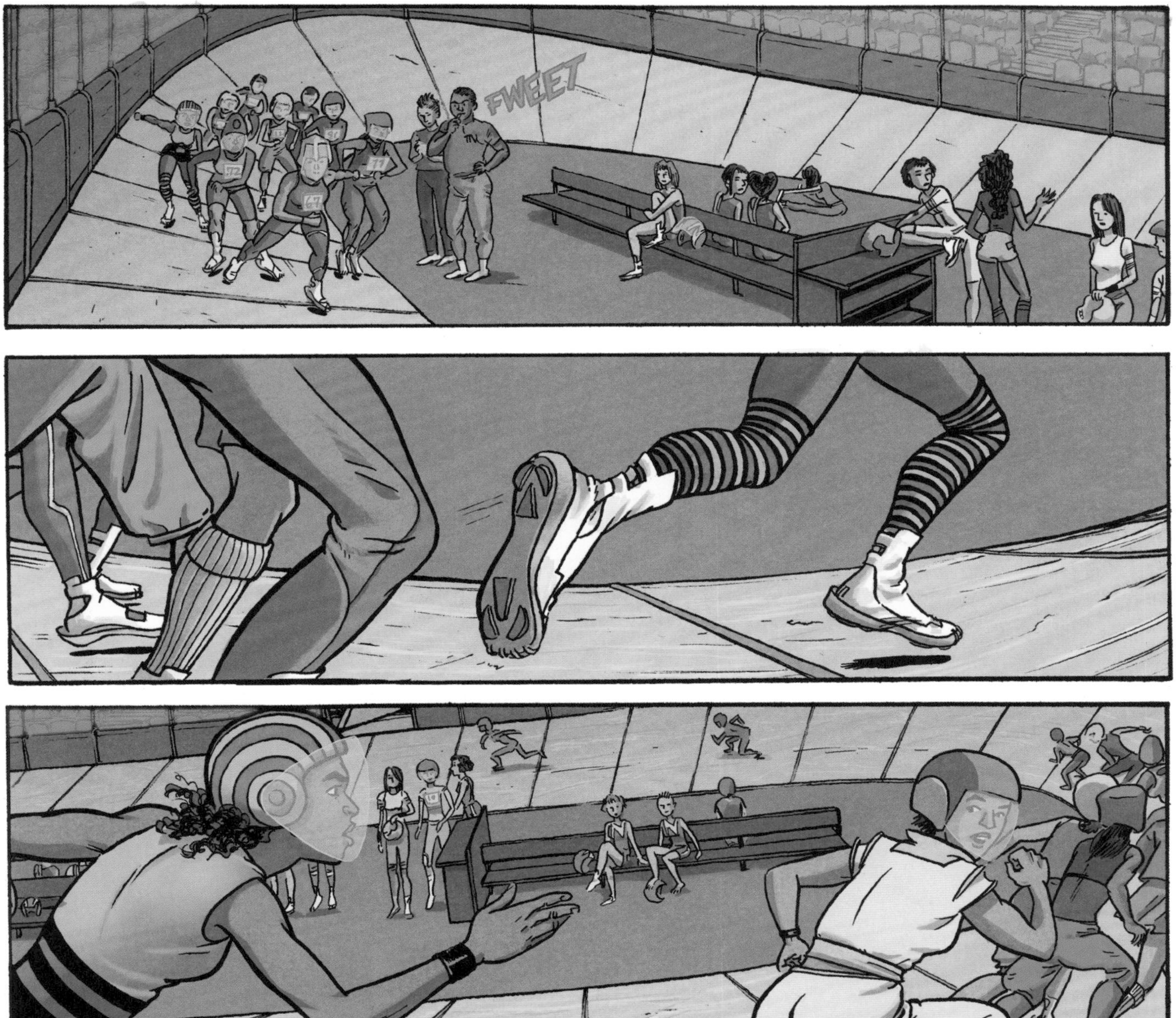
FWEET

*In derby, rookie players are called "fresh meat."

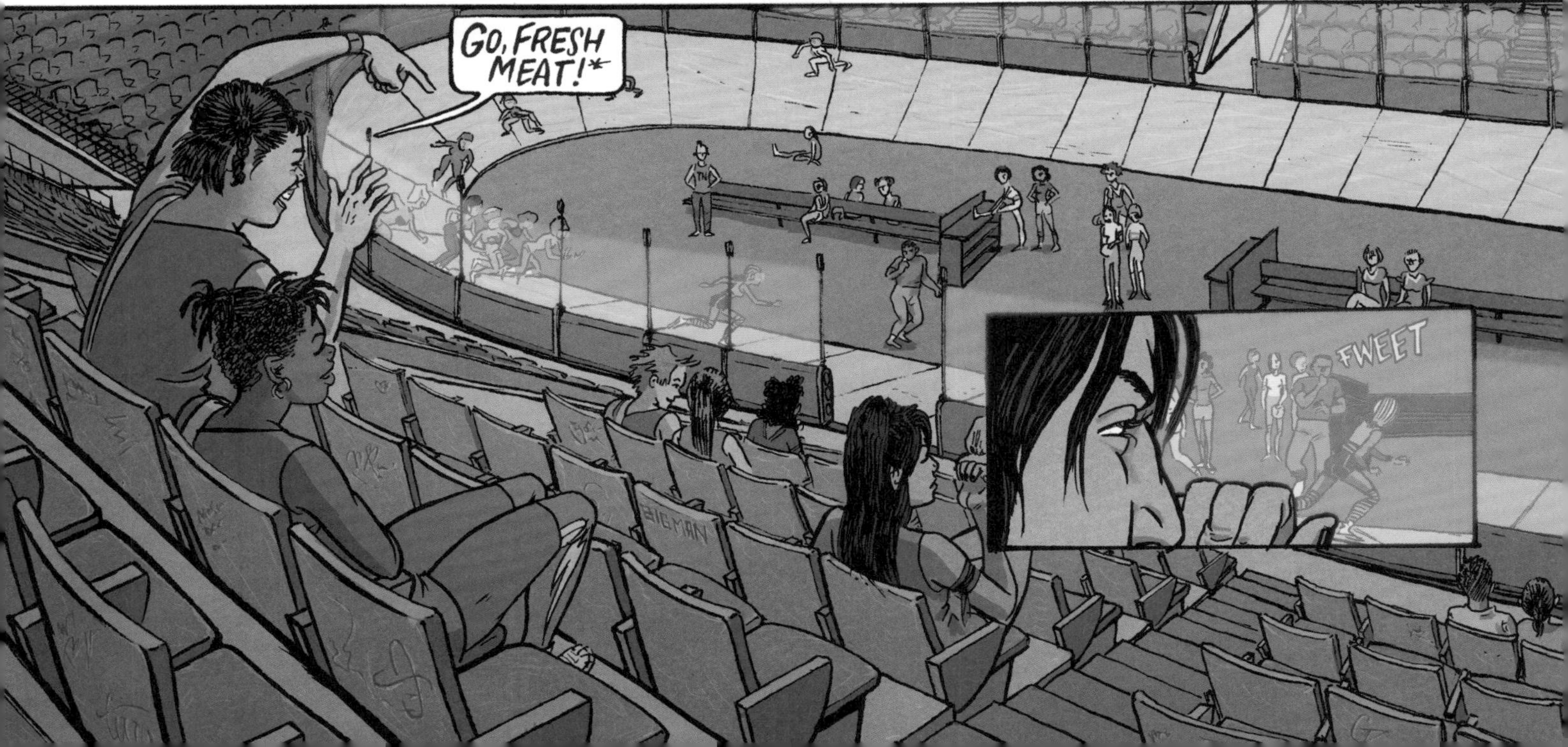
GO, FRESH MEAT!*
FWEET

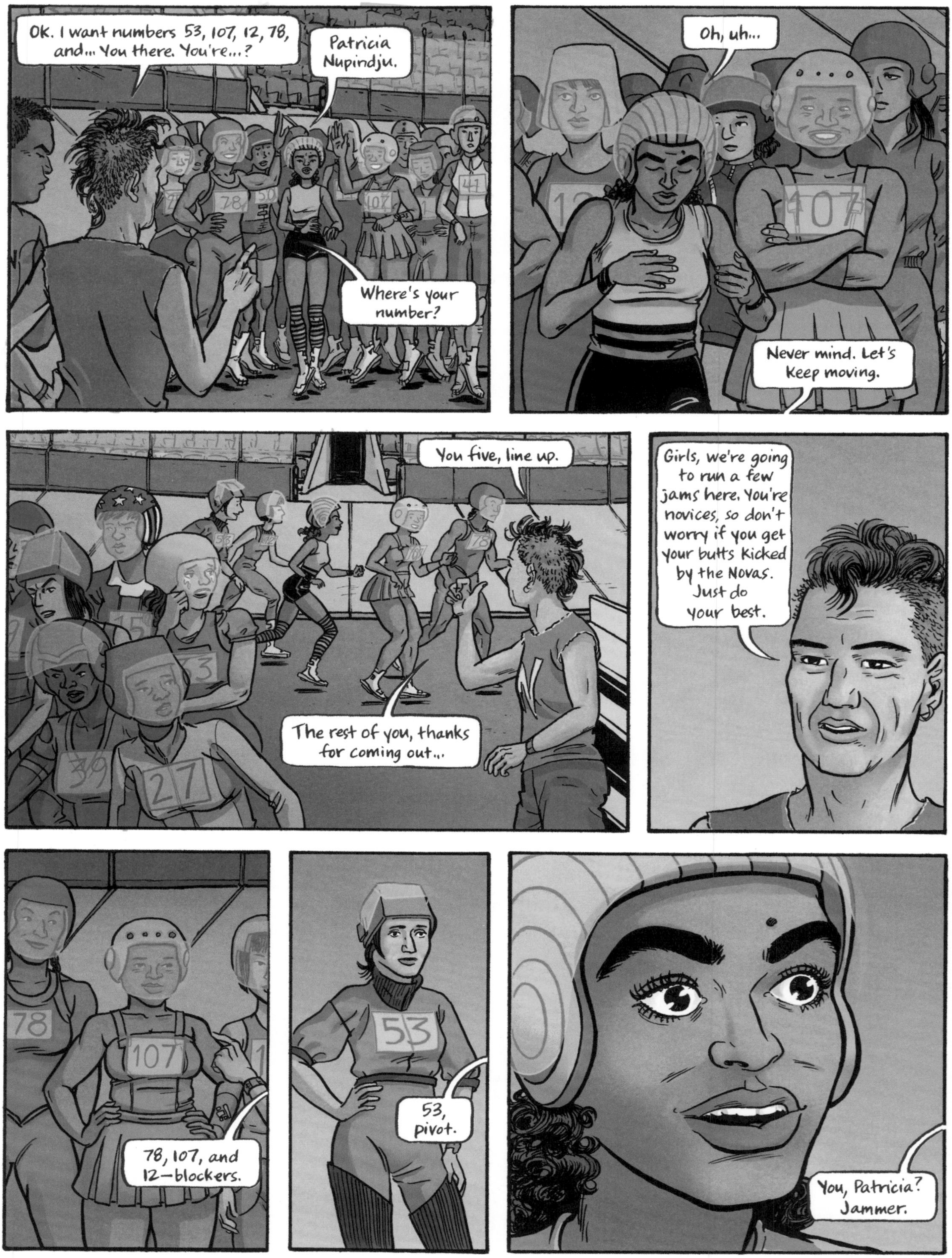
Ok. I want numbers 53, 107, 12, 78, and... You there. You're...?
Patricia Nupindju.
Where's your number?
Oh, uh...
Never mind. Let's keep moving.
You five, line up.
The rest of you, thanks for coming out...
Girls, we're going to run a few jams here. You're novices, so don't worry if you get your butts kicked by the Novas. Just do your best.
78, 107, and 12—blockers.
53, pivot.
You, Patricia? Jammer.

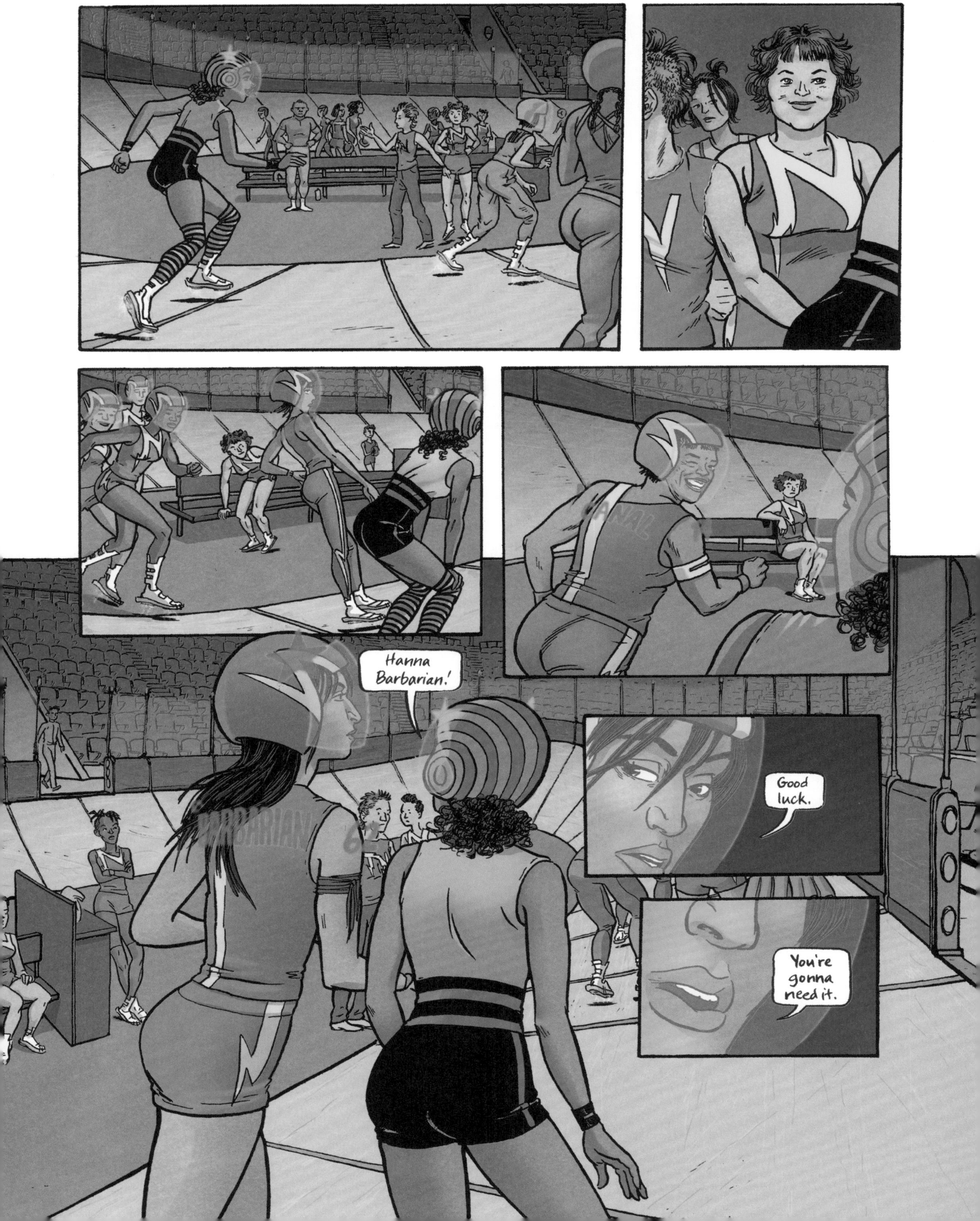
Hanna Barbarian!
Good luck.
You're gonna need it.

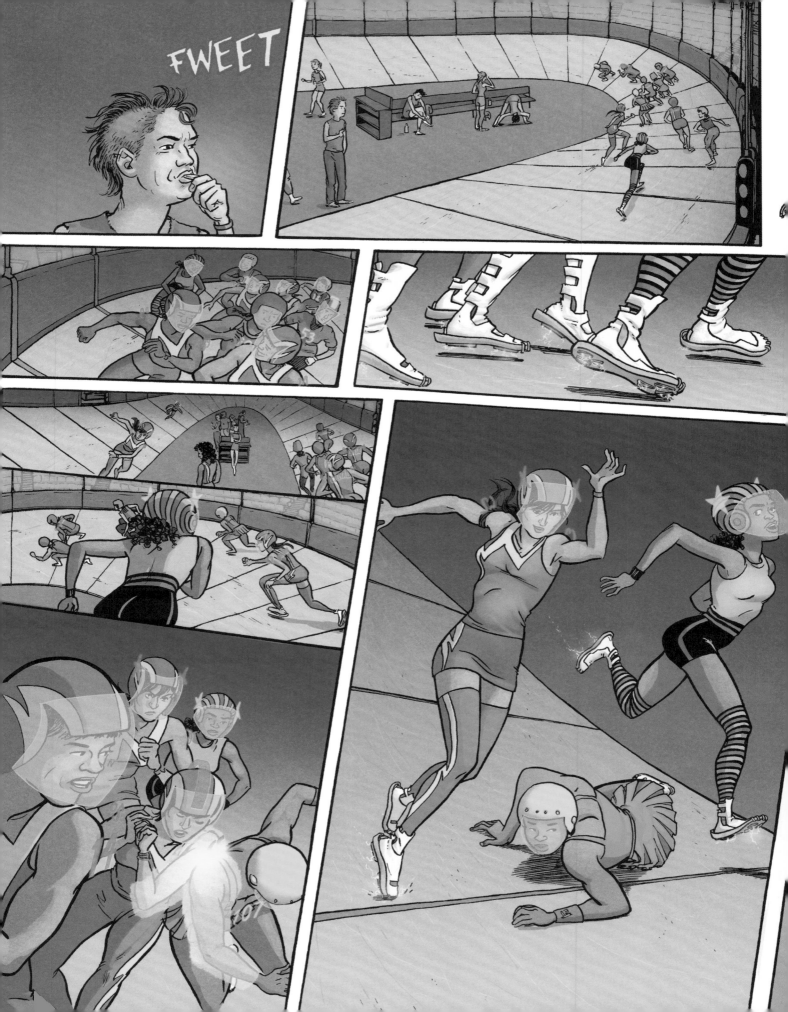

FWEET

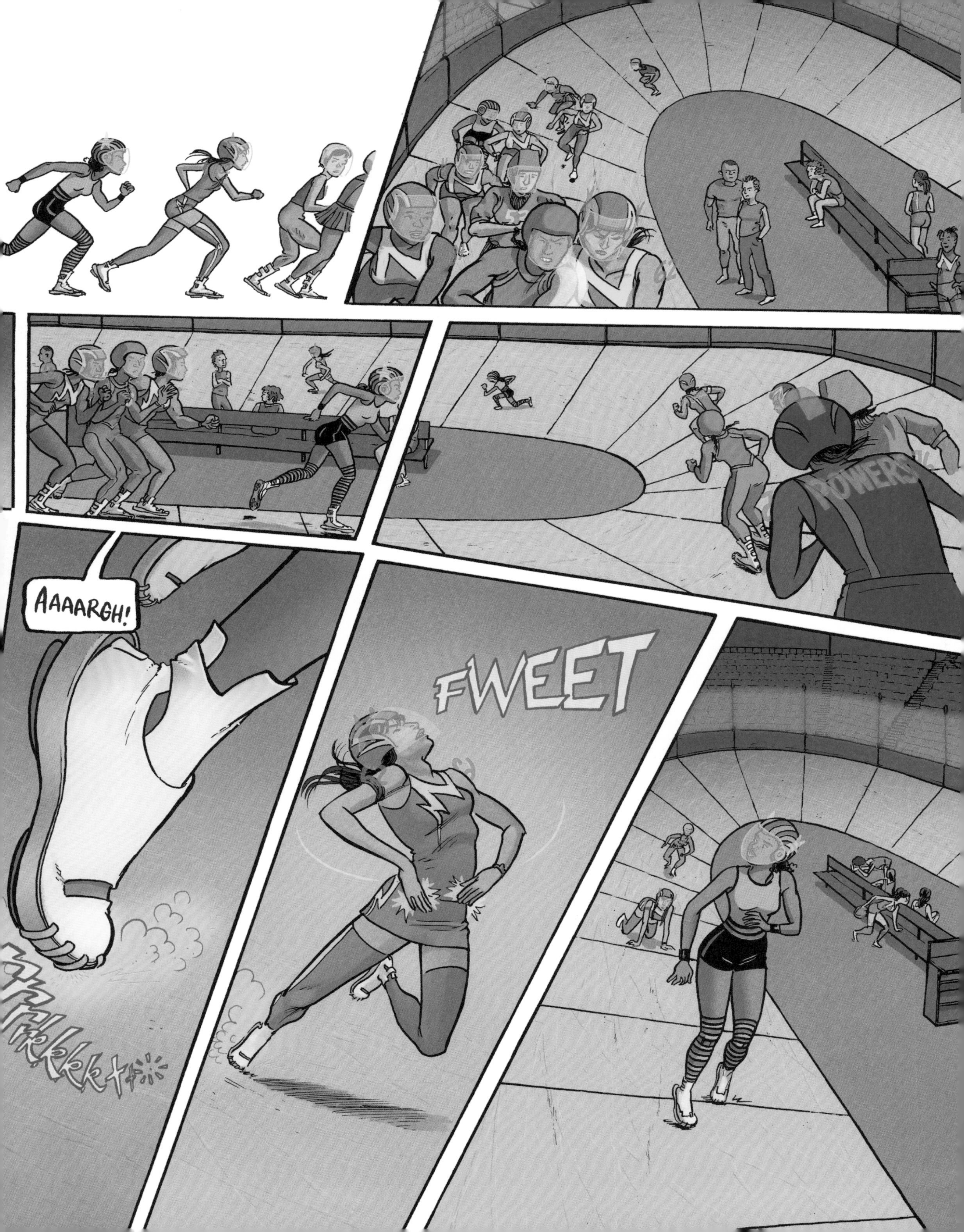
POWERS
AAAARGH!
FWEET

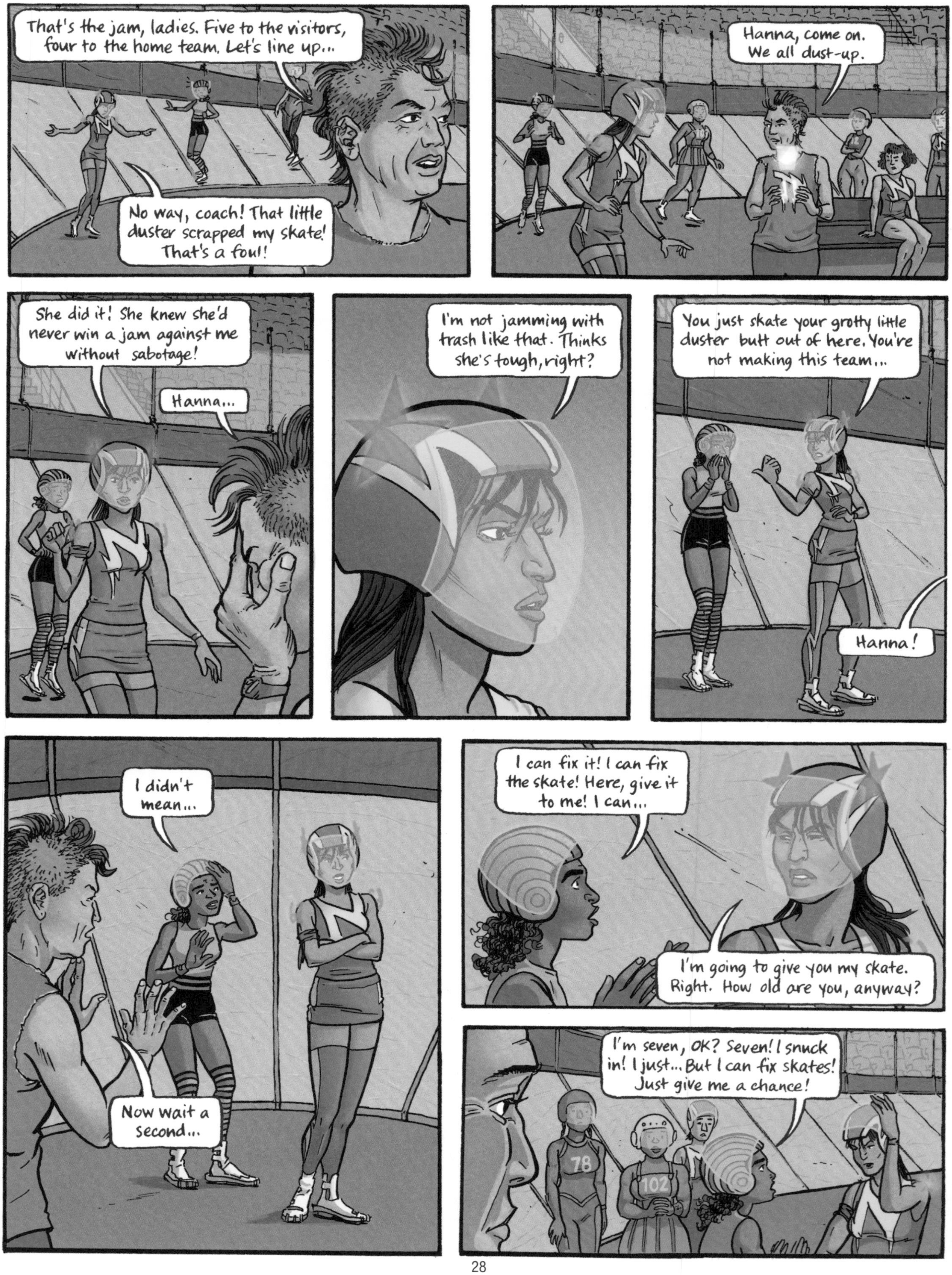
That's the jam, ladies. Five to the visitors, four to the home team. Let's line up...
No way, coach! That little duster scrapped my skate! That's a foul!
Hanna, come on. We all dust-up.
She did it! She knew she'd never win a jam against me without sabotage!
Hanna...
I'm not jamming with trash like that. Thinks she's tough, right?
You just skate your grotty little duster butt out of here. You're not making this team...
Hanna!
I didn't mean...
Now wait a second...
I can fix it! I can fix the skate! Here, give it to me! I can...
I'm going to give you my skate. Right. How old are you, anyway?
I'm seven, OK? Seven! I snuck in! I just... But I can fix skates! Just give me a chance!
78
102

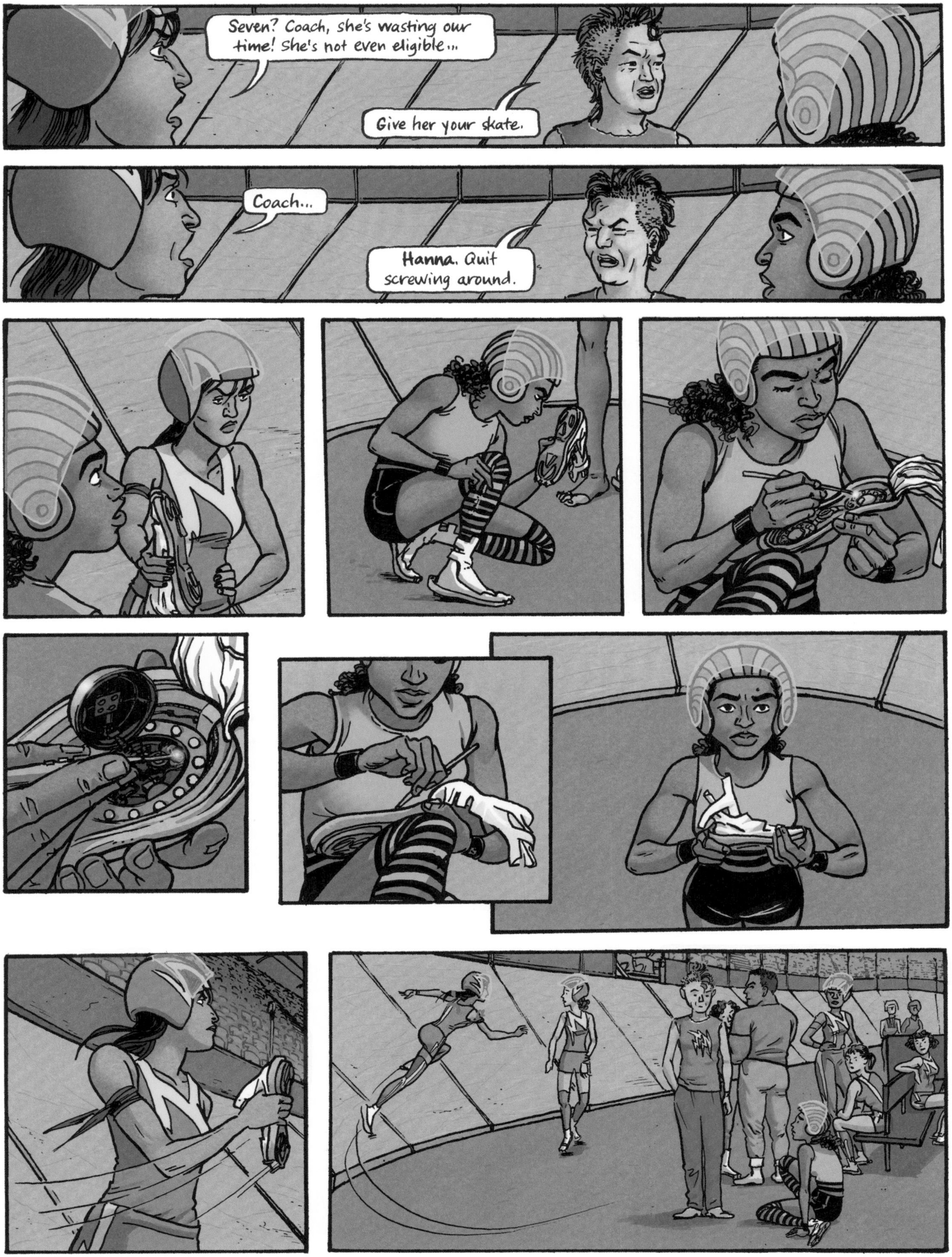
Seven? Coach, she's wasting our time! She's not even eligible...
Give her your skate.
Coach...
Hanna. Quit screwing around.

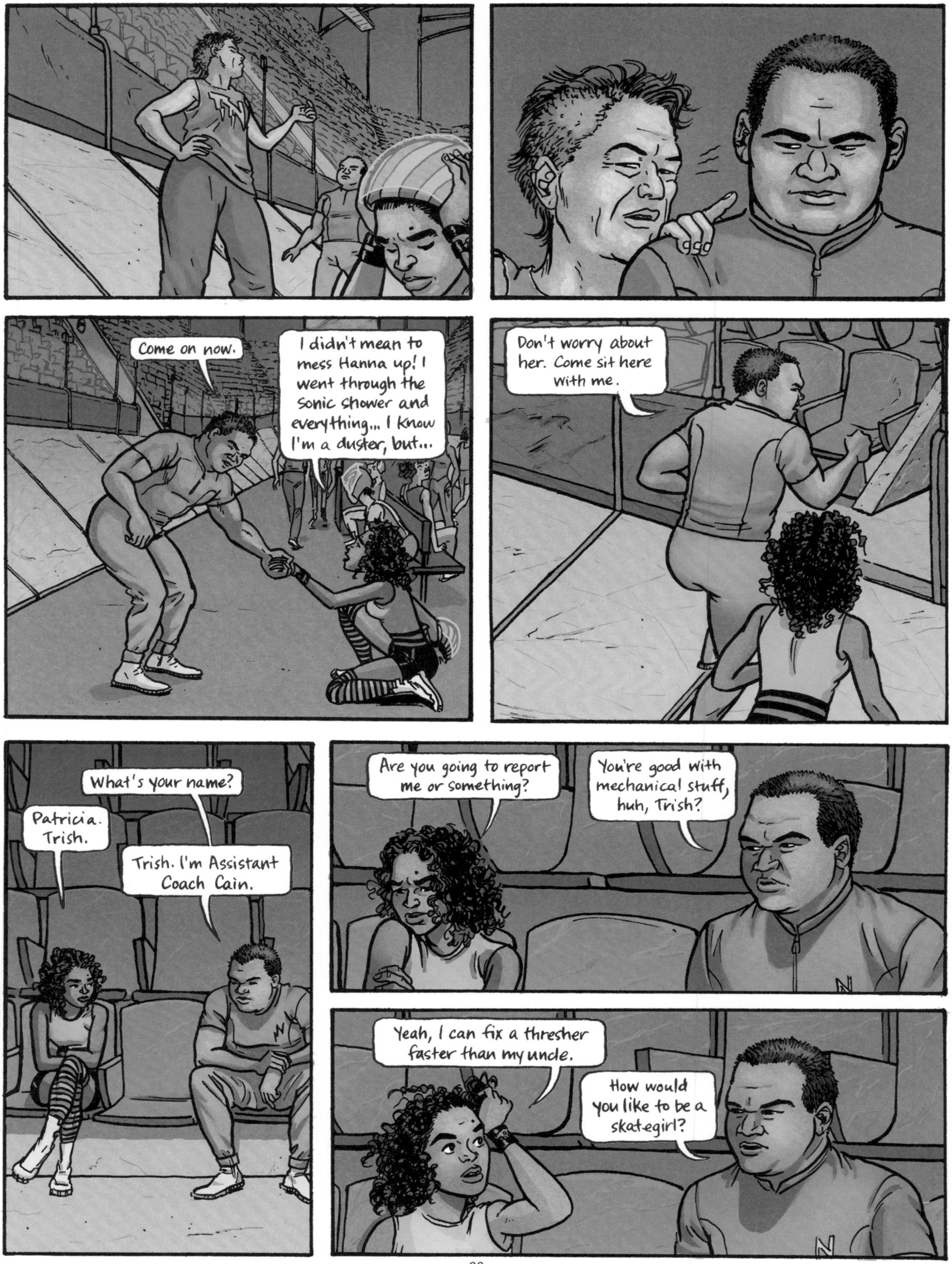
Come on now.
I didn't mean to mess Hanna up! I went through the sonic shower and everything... I know I'm a duster, but...
Don't worry about her. Come sit here with me.
What's your name?
Patricia. Trish.
Trish. I'm Assistant Coach Cain.
Are you going to report me or something?
You're good with mechanical stuff, huh, Trish?
Yeah, I can fix a thresher faster than my uncle.
How would you like to be a skategirl?

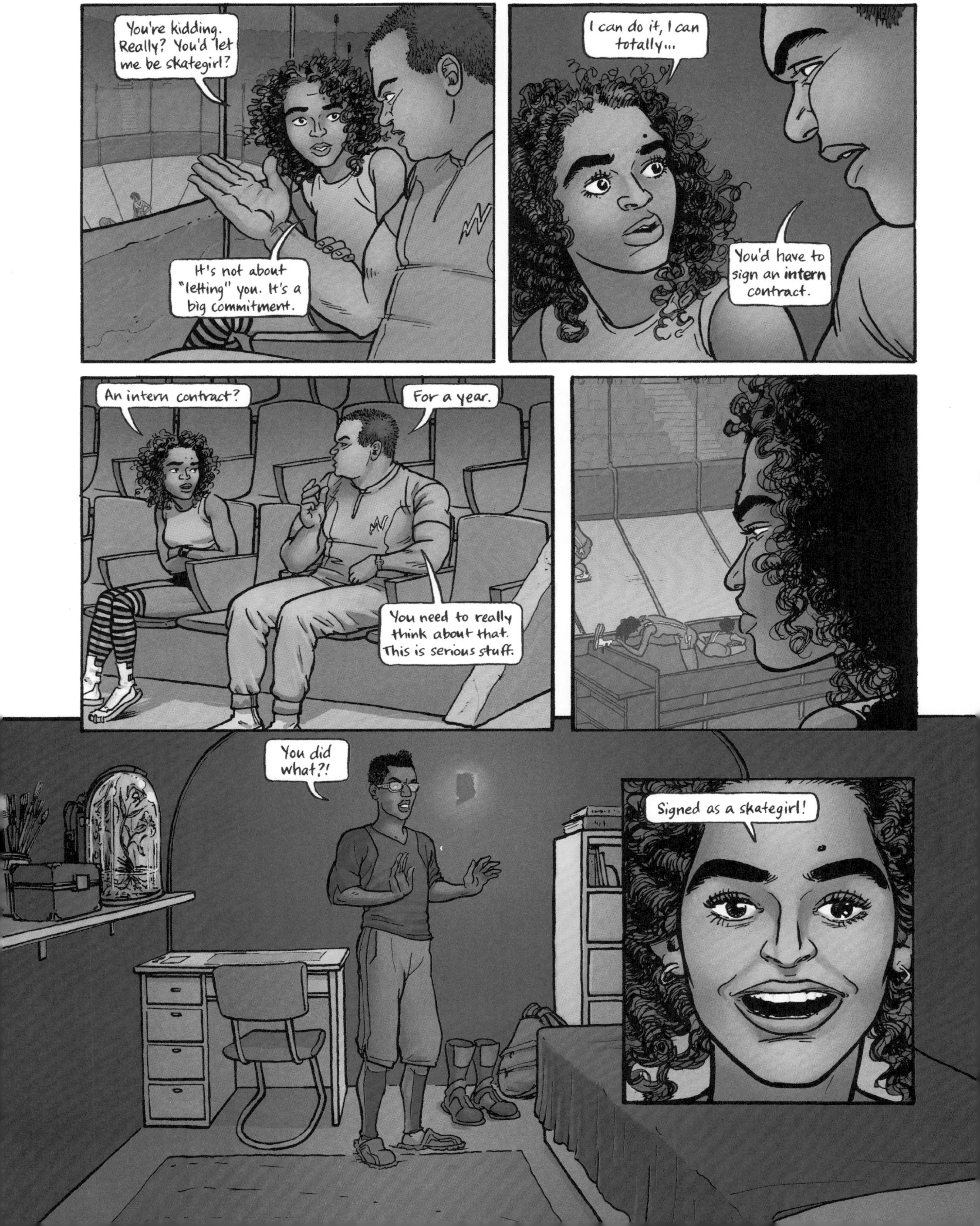
You're kidding. Really? You'd let me be skategirl?
It's not about "letting" you. It's a big commitment.
I can do it, I can totally...
You'd have to sign an **intern** contract.
An intern contract?
For a year.
You need to really think about that. This is serious stuff.
You did what?!
Signed as a skategirl!

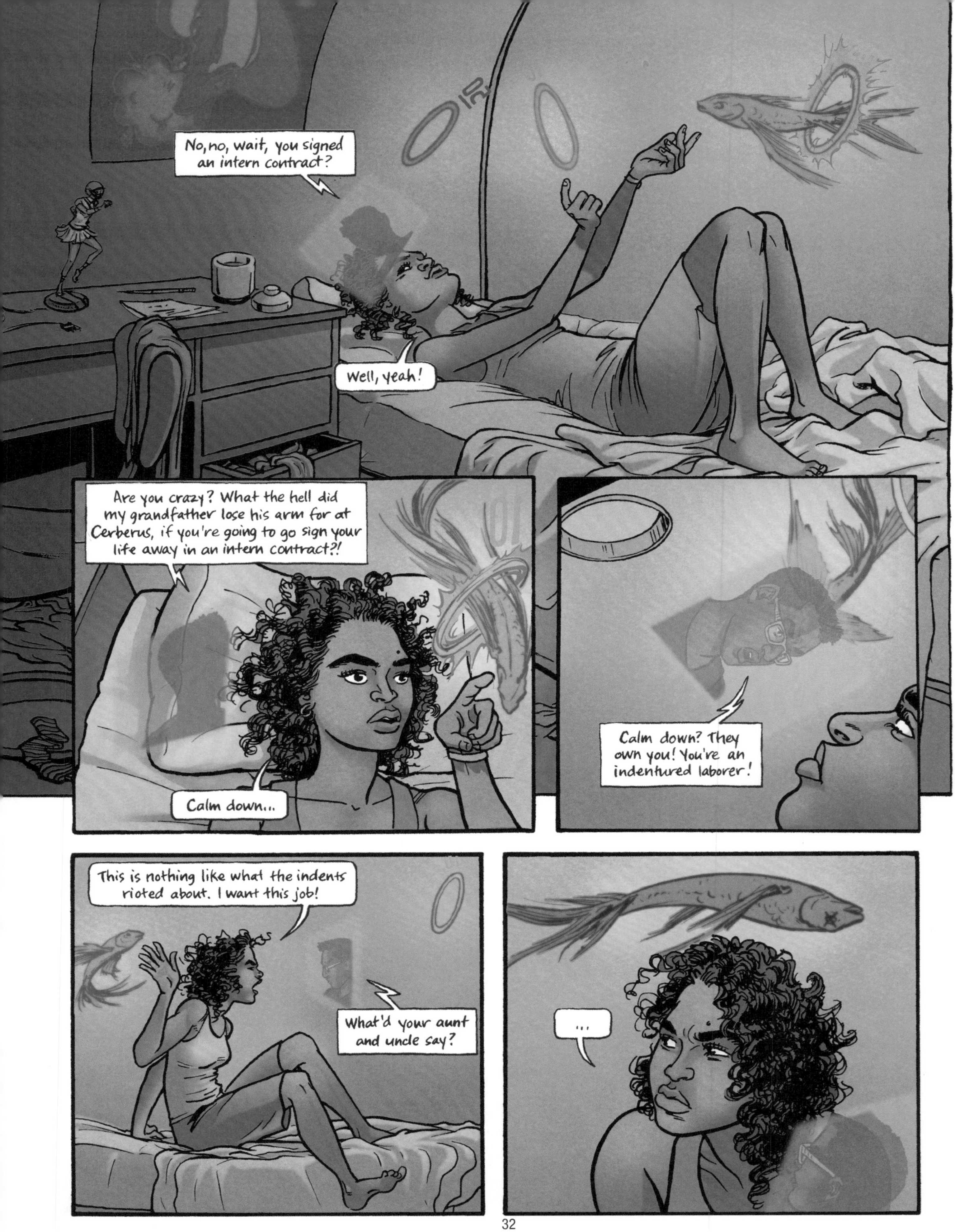
No, no, wait, you signed an intern contract?
Well, yeah!
Are you crazy? What the hell did my grandfather lose his arm for at Cerberus, if you're going to go sign your life away in an intern contract?!
Calm down...
Calm down? They own you! You're an indentured laborer!
This is nothing like what the indents rioted about. I want this job!
What'd your aunt and uncle say?
...

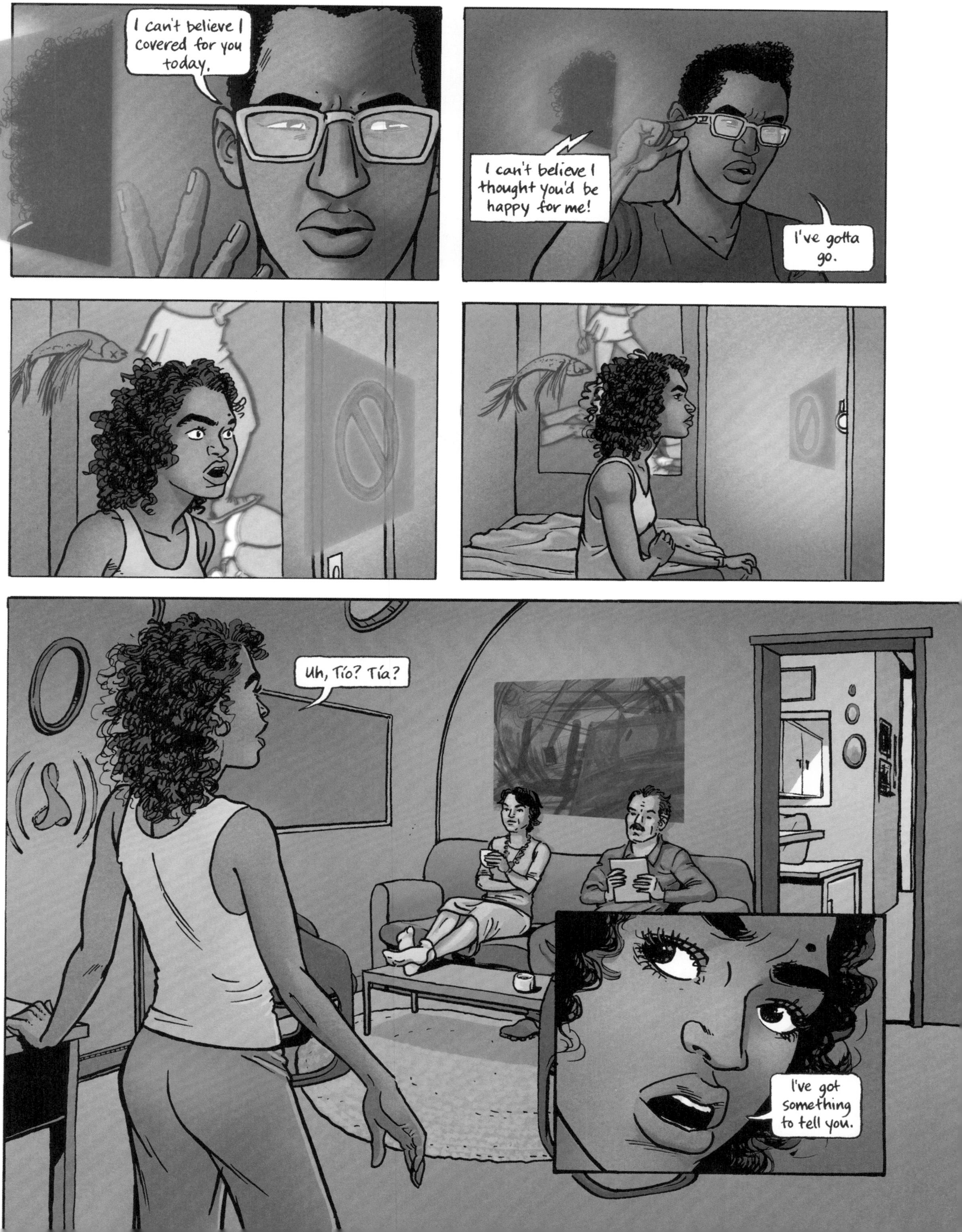
I can't believe I covered for you today.
I can't believe I thought you'd be happy for me!
I've gotta go.
Uh, Tío? Tía?
I've got something to tell you.

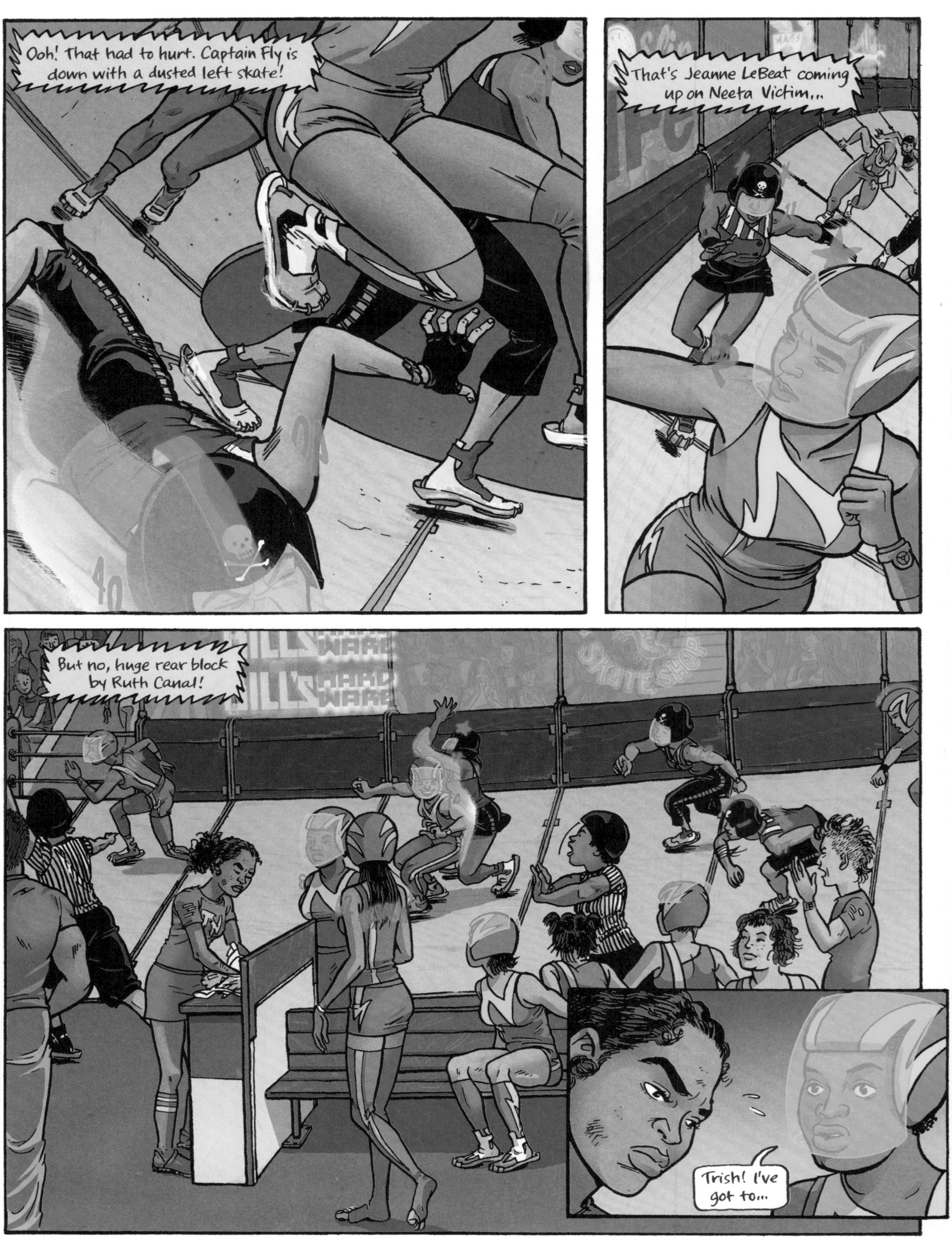
Ooh! That had to hurt. Captain Fly is down with a dusted left skate!
That's Jeanne LeBeat coming up on Neeta Victim...
But no, huge rear block by Ruth Canal!
SKATE SHOP
Trish! I've got to...

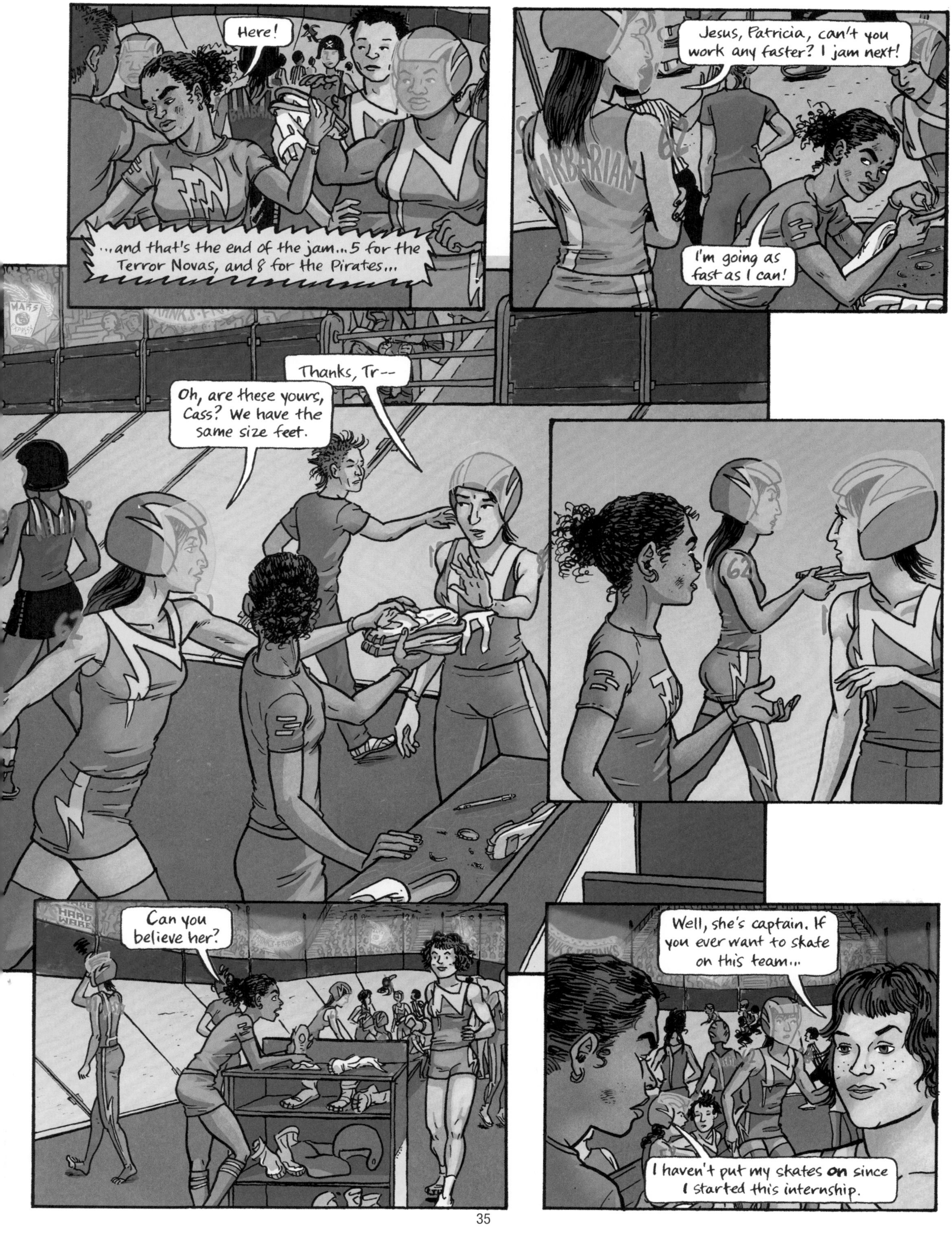
Here!
...and that's the end of the jam... 5 for the Terror Novas, and 8 for the Pirates...
Jesus, Patricia, can't you work any faster? I jam next!
I'm going as fast as I can!
BARBARIAN
Oh, are these yours, Cass? We have the same size feet.
Thanks, Tr--
Can you believe her?
Well, she's captain. If you ever want to skate on this team...
I haven't put my skates **on** since I started this internship.

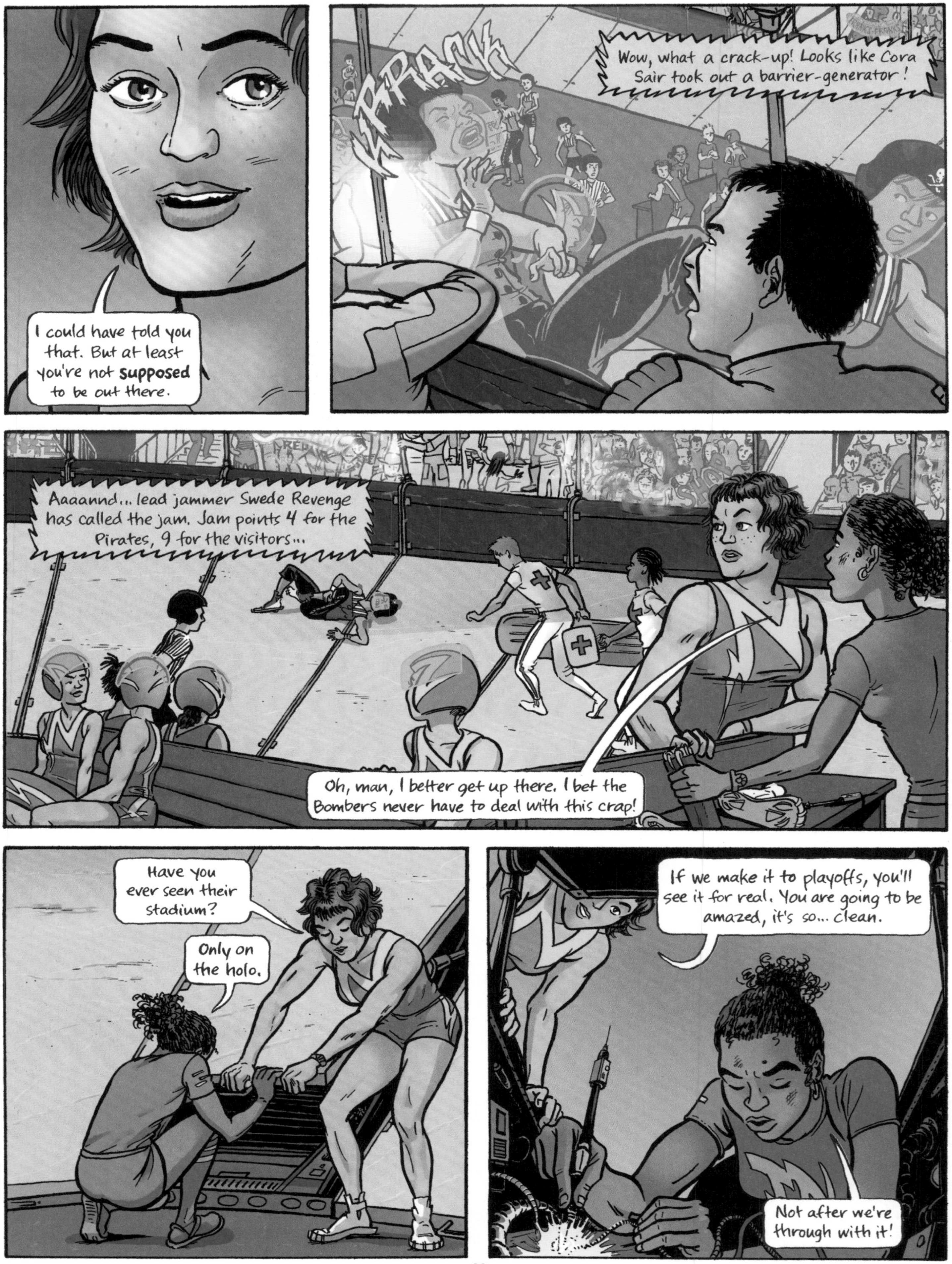
I could have told you that. But at least you're not **supposed** to be out there.
Wow, what a crack-up! Looks like Cora Sair took out a barrier-generator!
Aaaannd... lead jammer Swede Revenge has called the jam. Jam points 4 for the Pirates, 9 for the visitors...
Oh, man, I better get up there. I bet the Bombers never have to deal with this crap!
Have you ever seen their stadium?
Only on the holo.
If we make it to playoffs, you'll see it for real. You are going to be amazed, it's so... clean.
Not after we're through with it!

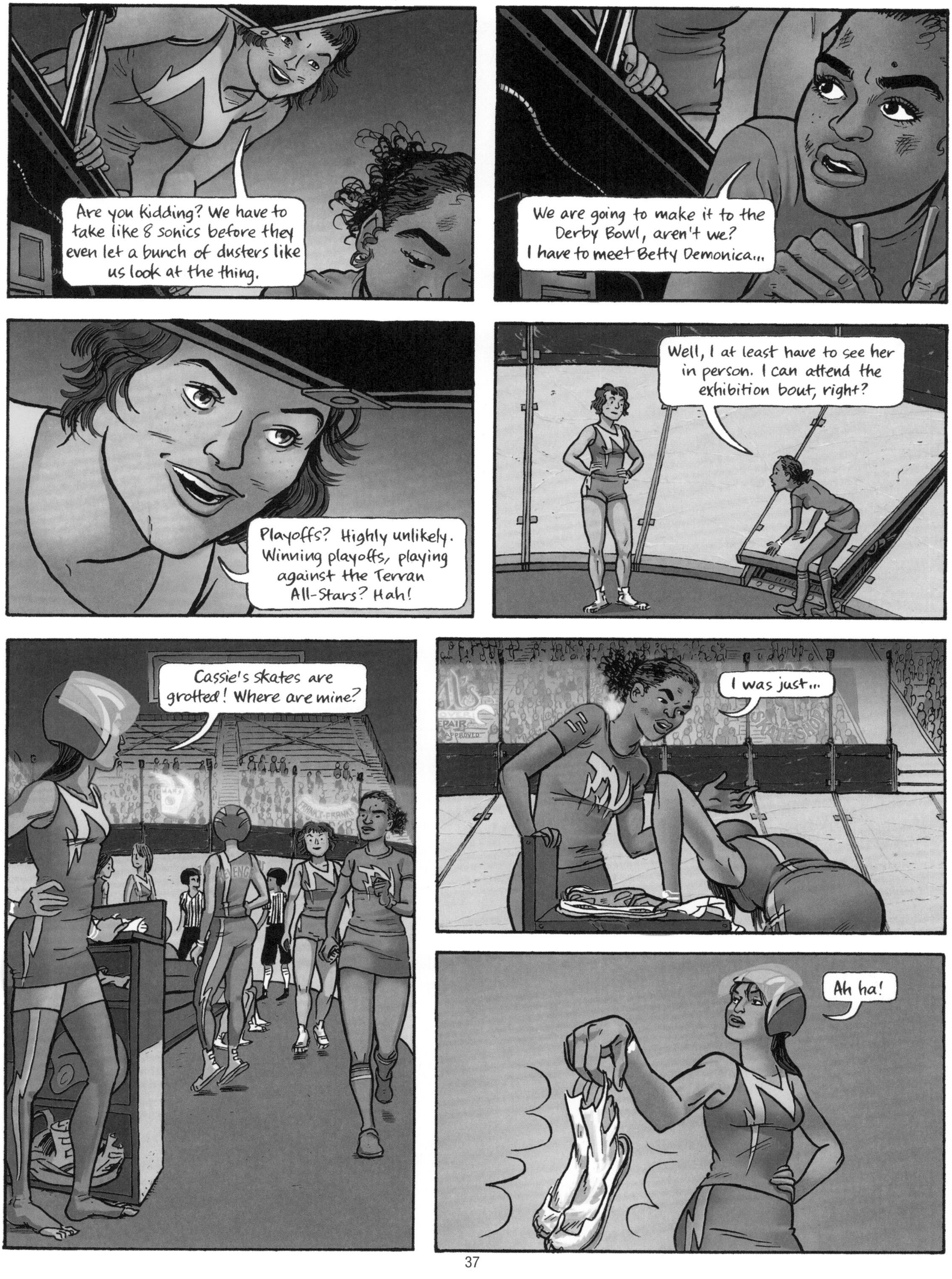
Are you kidding? We have to take like 8 sonics before they even let a bunch of dusters like us look at the thing.
We are going to make it to the Derby Bowl, aren't we? I have to meet Betty Demonica...
Playoffs? Highly unlikely. Winning playoffs, playing against the Terran All-Stars? Hah!
Well, I at least have to see her in person. I can attend the exhibition bout, right?
Cassie's skates are grotted! Where are mine?
I was just...
Ah ha!

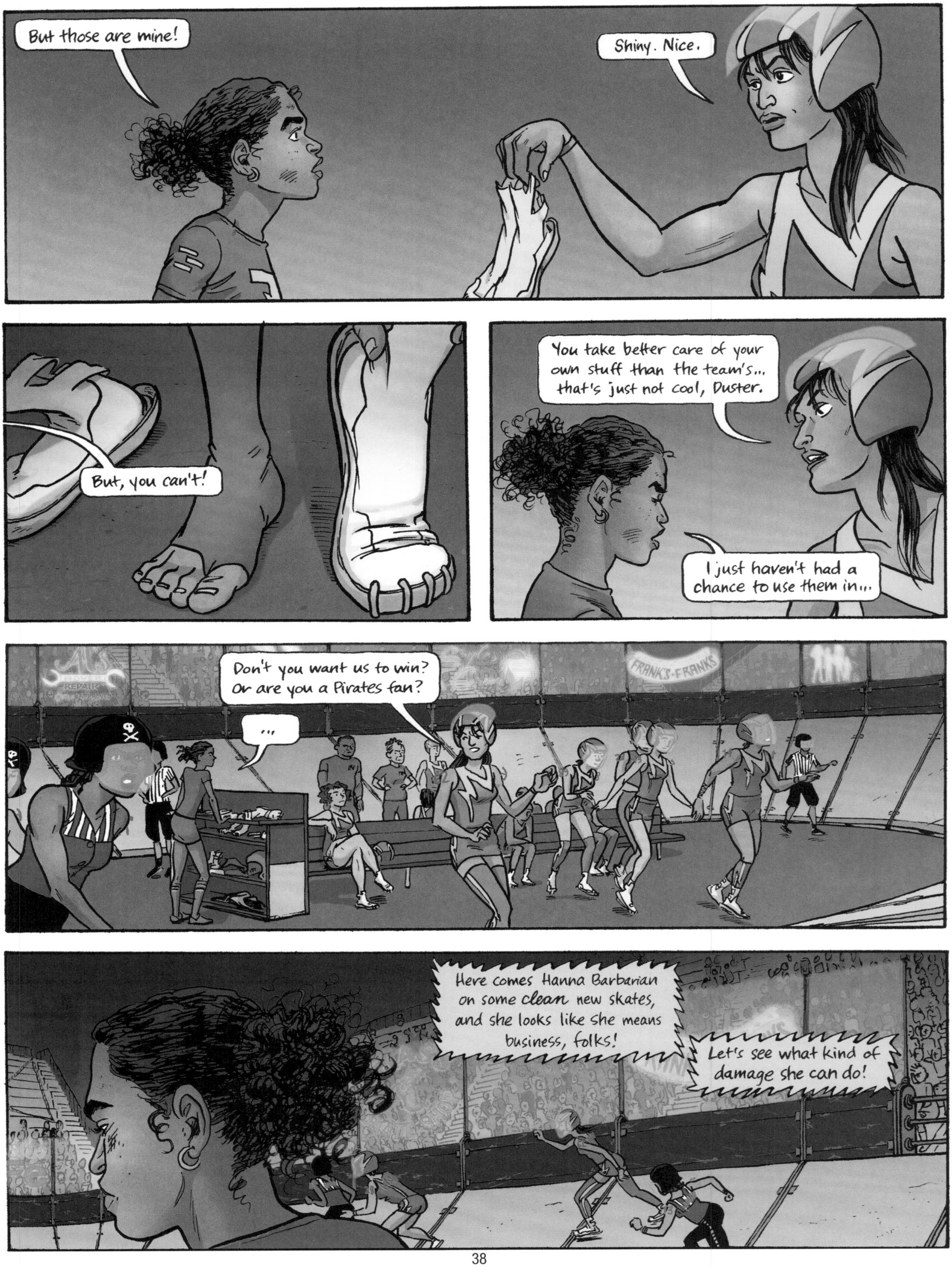
But those are mine!
Shiny. Nice.
But, you can't!
You take better care of your own stuff than the team's... that's just not cool, Duster.
I just haven't had a chance to use them in...
Don't you want us to win? Or are you a Pirates fan?
...
FRANK'S FRANKS
Here comes Hanna Barbarian on some clean new skates, and she looks like she means business, folks!
Let's see what kind of damage she can do!

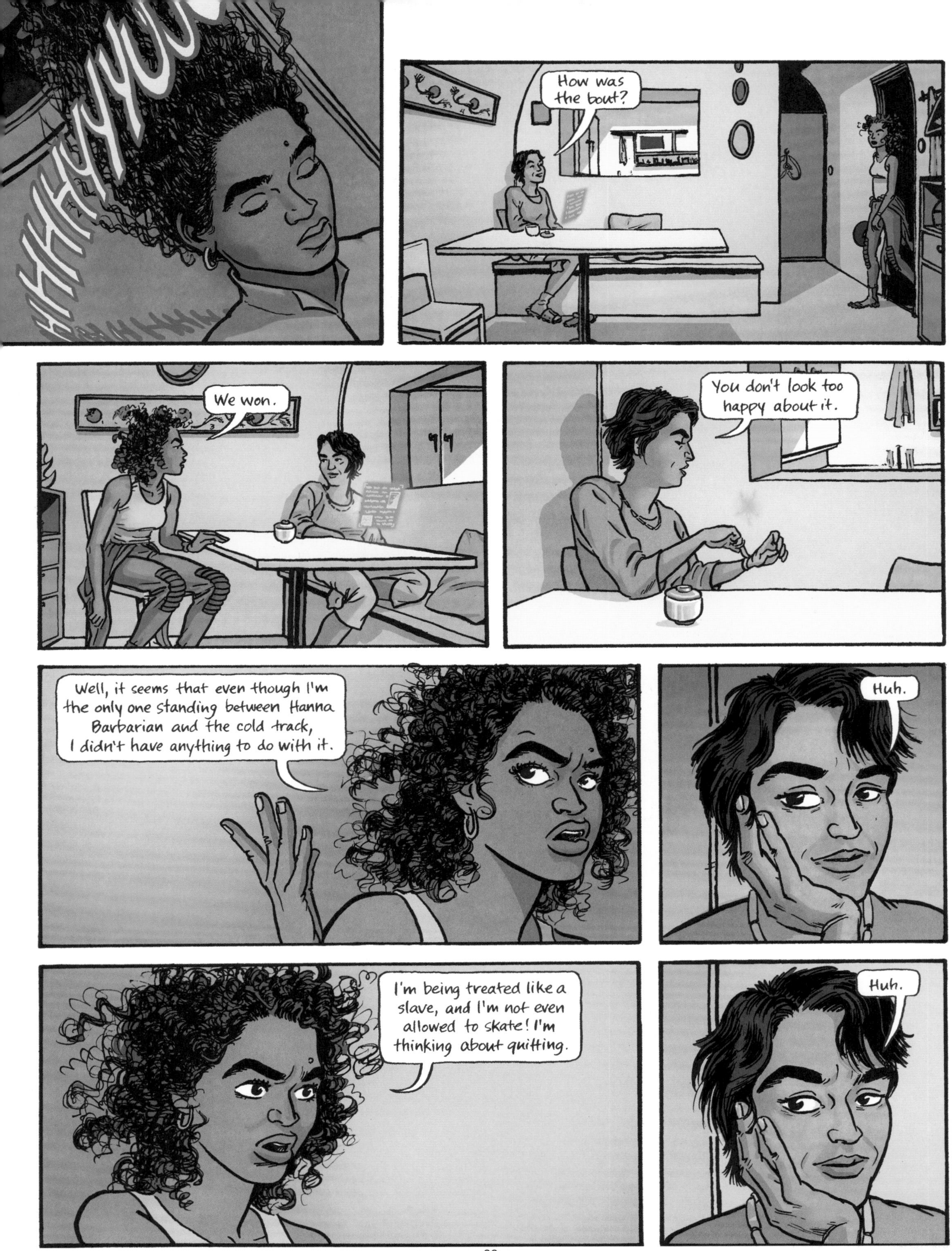
How was the bout?
We won.
You don't look too happy about it.
Well, it seems that even though I'm the only one standing between Hanna Barbarian and the cold track, I didn't have anything to do with it.
Huh.
I'm being treated like a slave, and I'm not even allowed to skate! I'm thinking about quitting.
Huh.

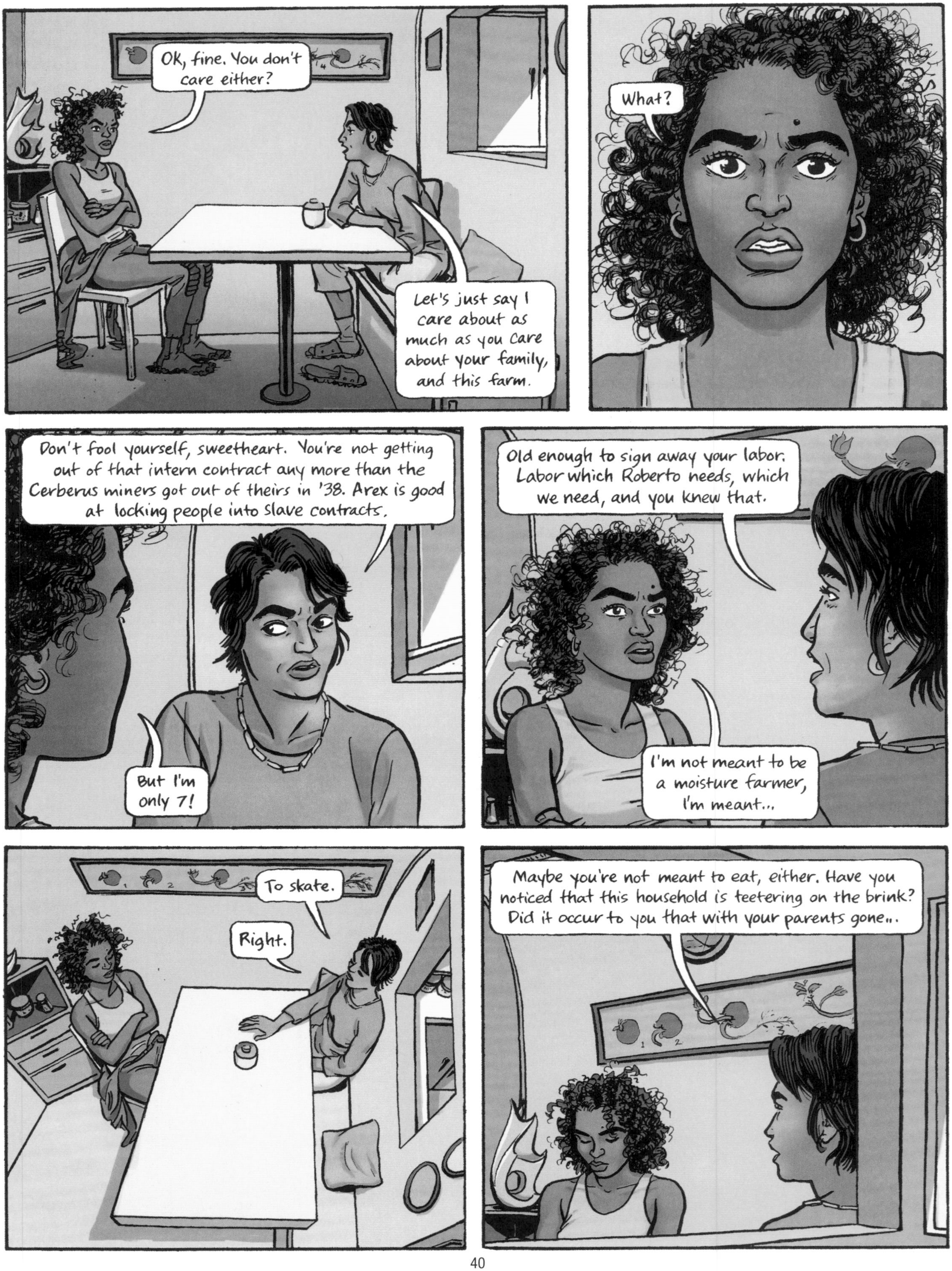
Ok, fine. You don't care either?
Let's just say I care about as much as you care about your family, and this farm.
What?
Don't fool yourself, sweetheart. You're not getting out of that intern contract any more than the Cerberus miners got out of theirs in '38. Arex is good at locking people into slave contracts.
But I'm only 7!
Old enough to sign away your labor. Labor which Roberto needs, which we need, and you knew that.
I'm not meant to be a moisture farmer, I'm meant...
To skate.
Right.
Maybe you're not meant to eat, either. Have you noticed that this household is teetering on the brink? Did it occur to you that with your parents gone...

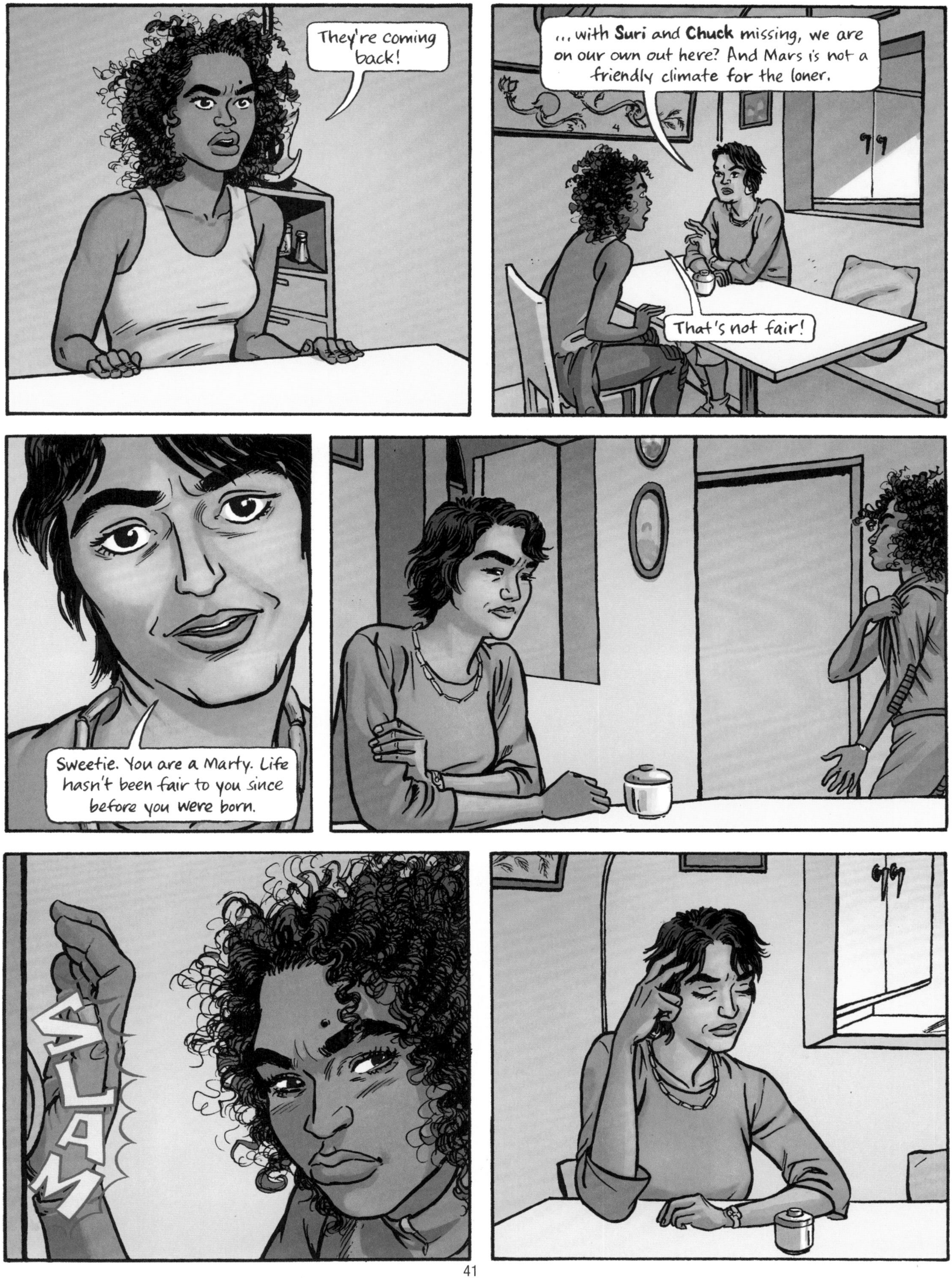
They're coming back!
...with Suri and Chuck missing, we are on our own out here? And Mars is not a friendly climate for the loner.
That's not fair!
Sweetie. You are a Marty. Life hasn't been fair to you since before you were born.
SLAM

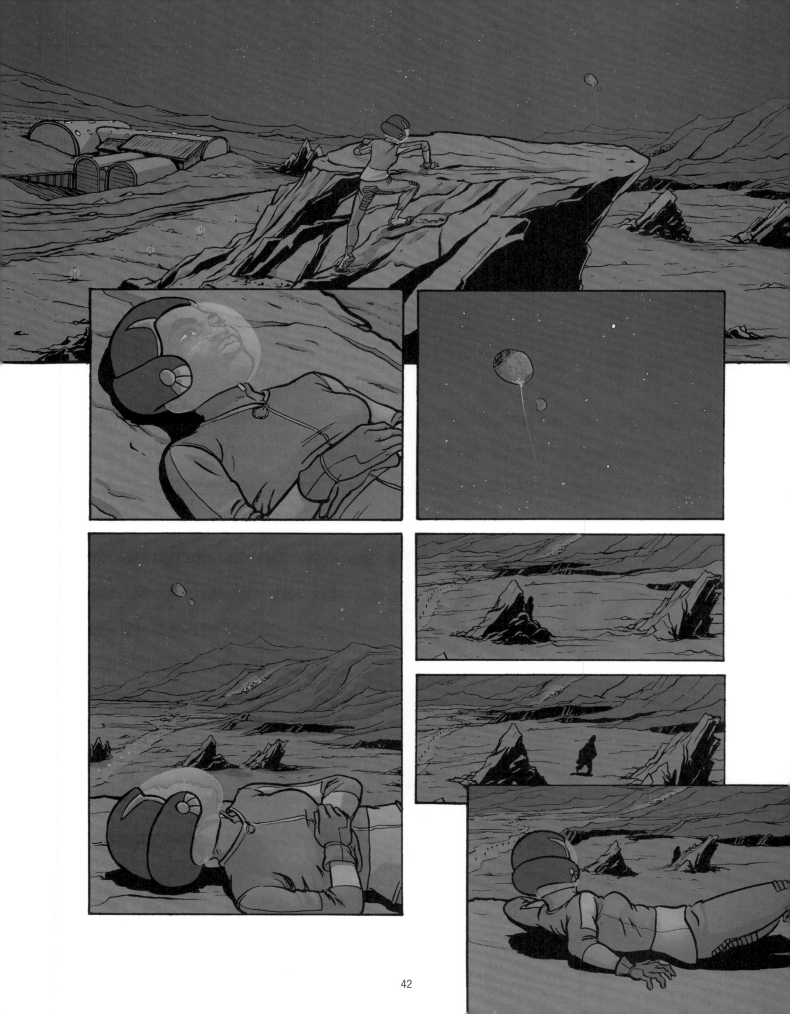

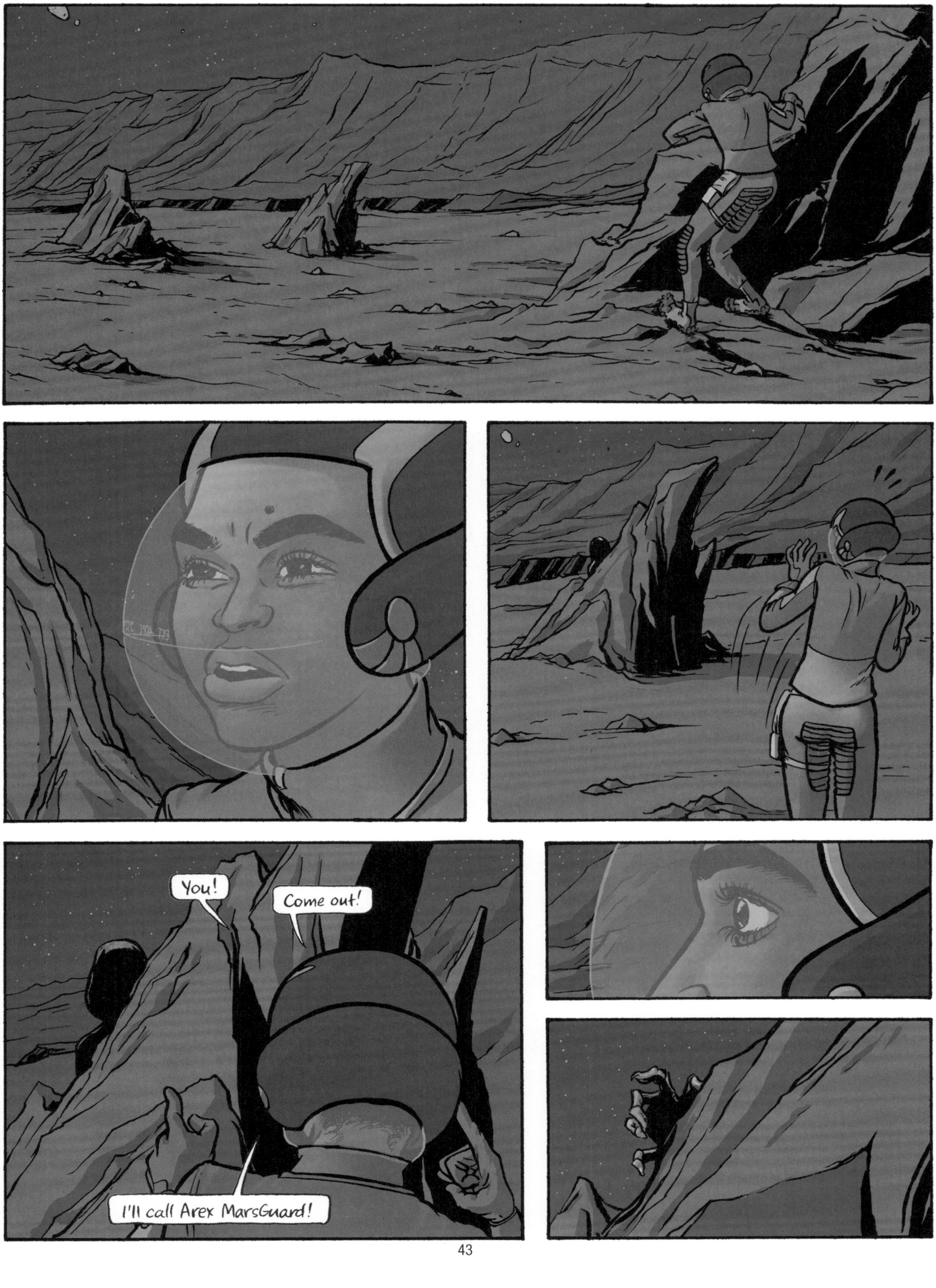
You!
Come out!
I'll call Arex MarsGuard!

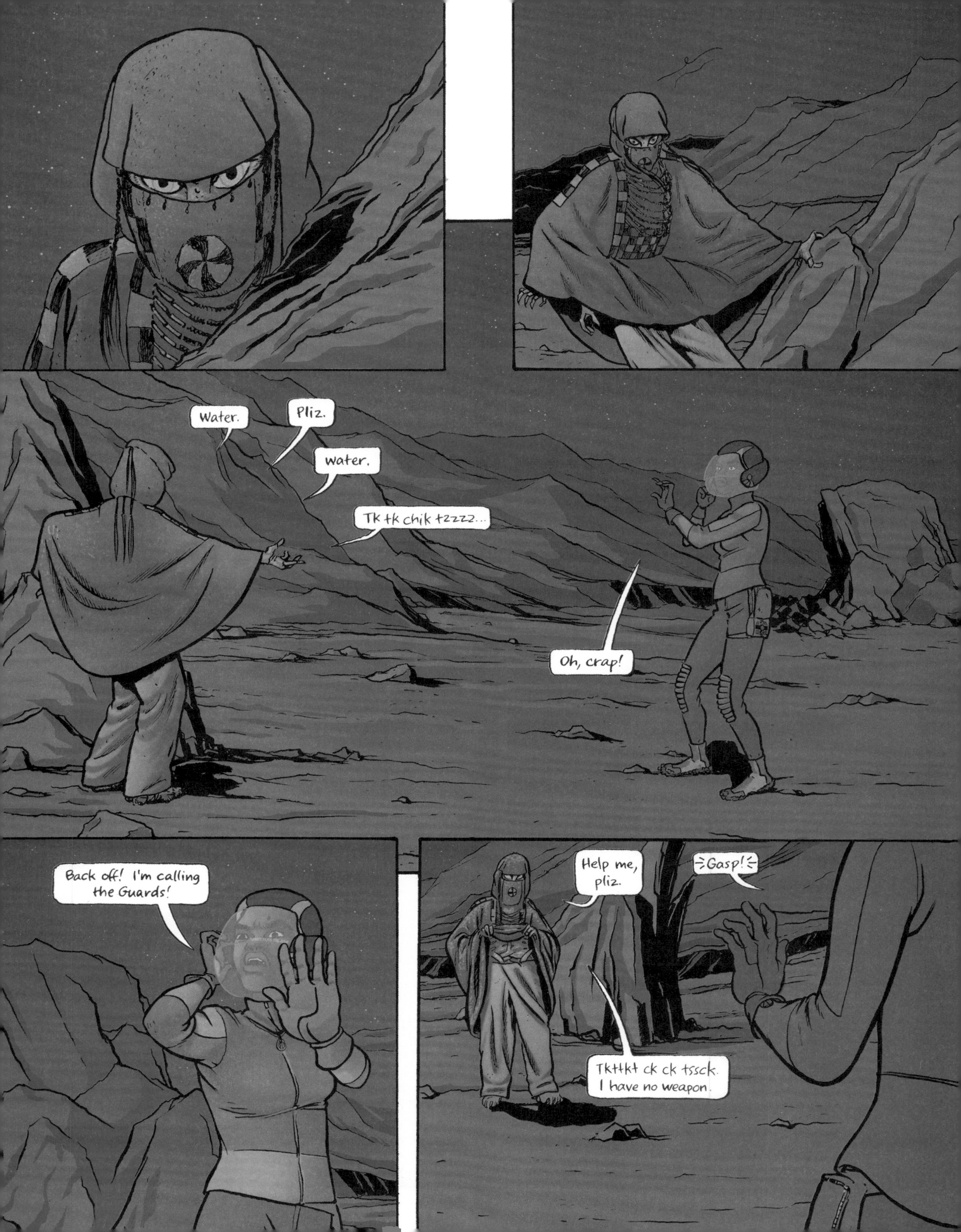
Water.
Pliz.
water.
Tk tk chik tzzzz...
Oh, crap!
Back off! I'm calling the Guards!
Help me, pliz.
Gasp!
Tkttkt ck ck tssck. I have no weapon.

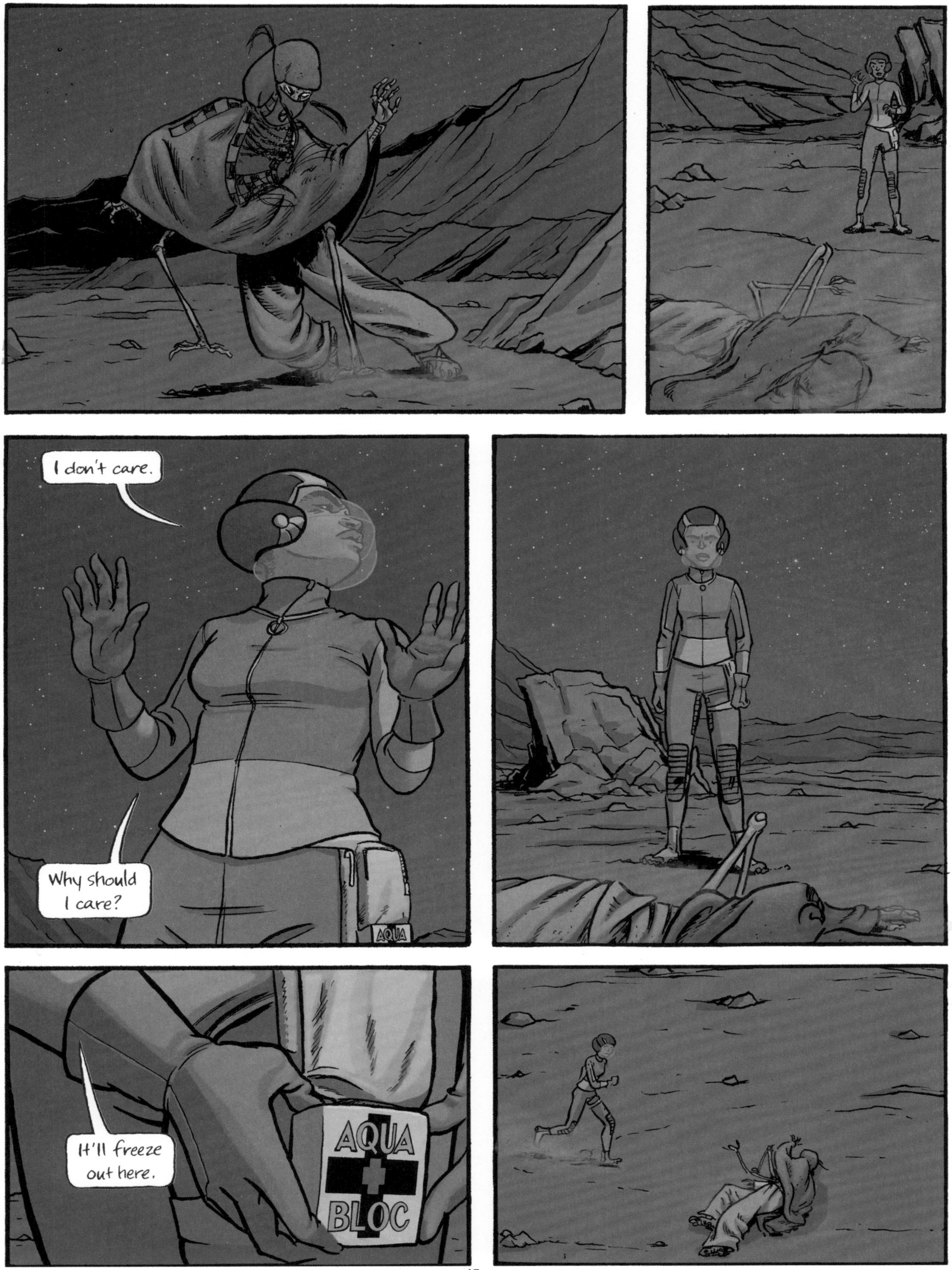
I don't care.
Why should I care?
AQUA
It'll freeze out here.
AQUA BLOC

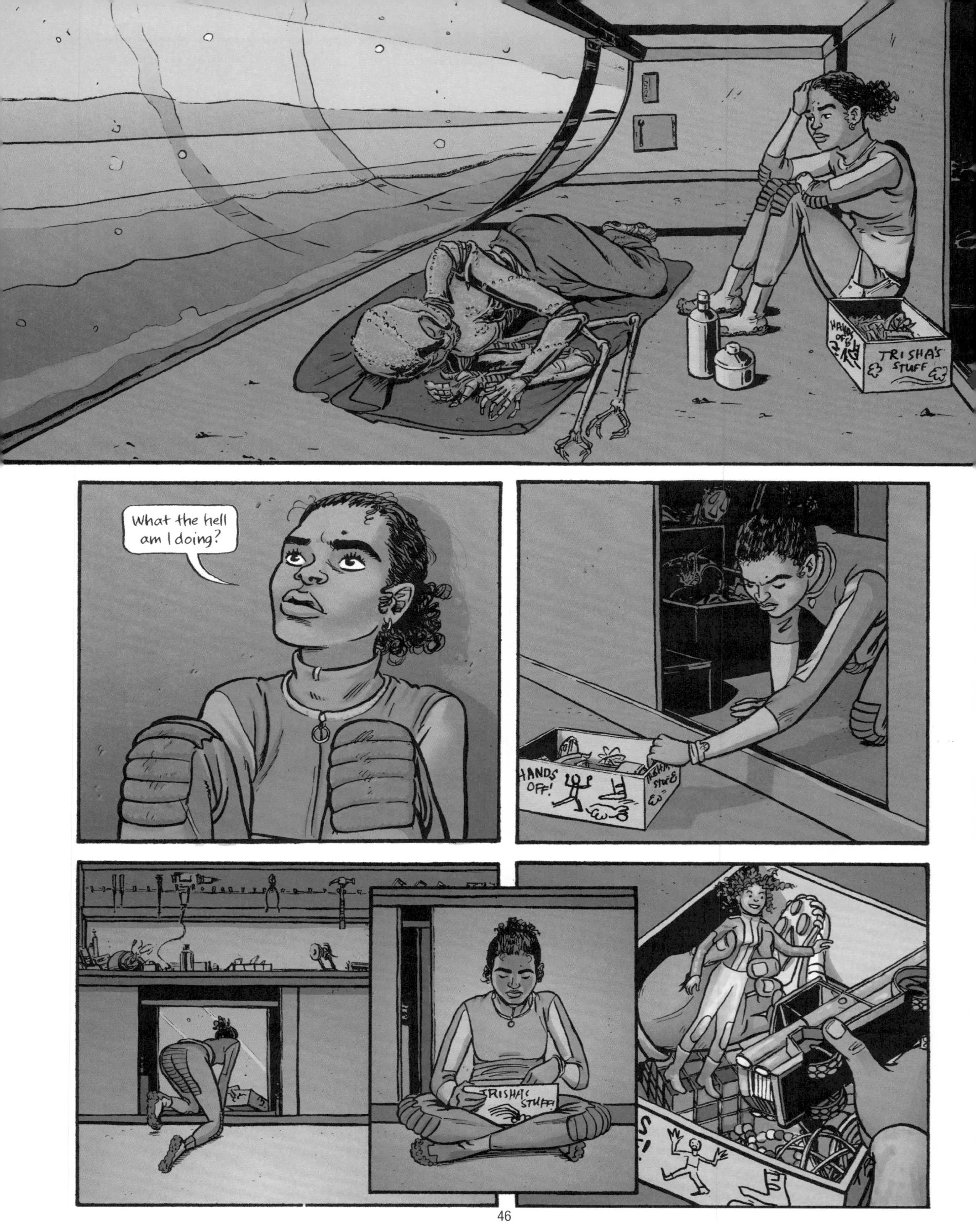
HANDS OFF
TRISHA'S STUFF
What the hell am I doing?
HANDS OFF!
TRISHA'S STUFF
TRISHA'S STUFF!

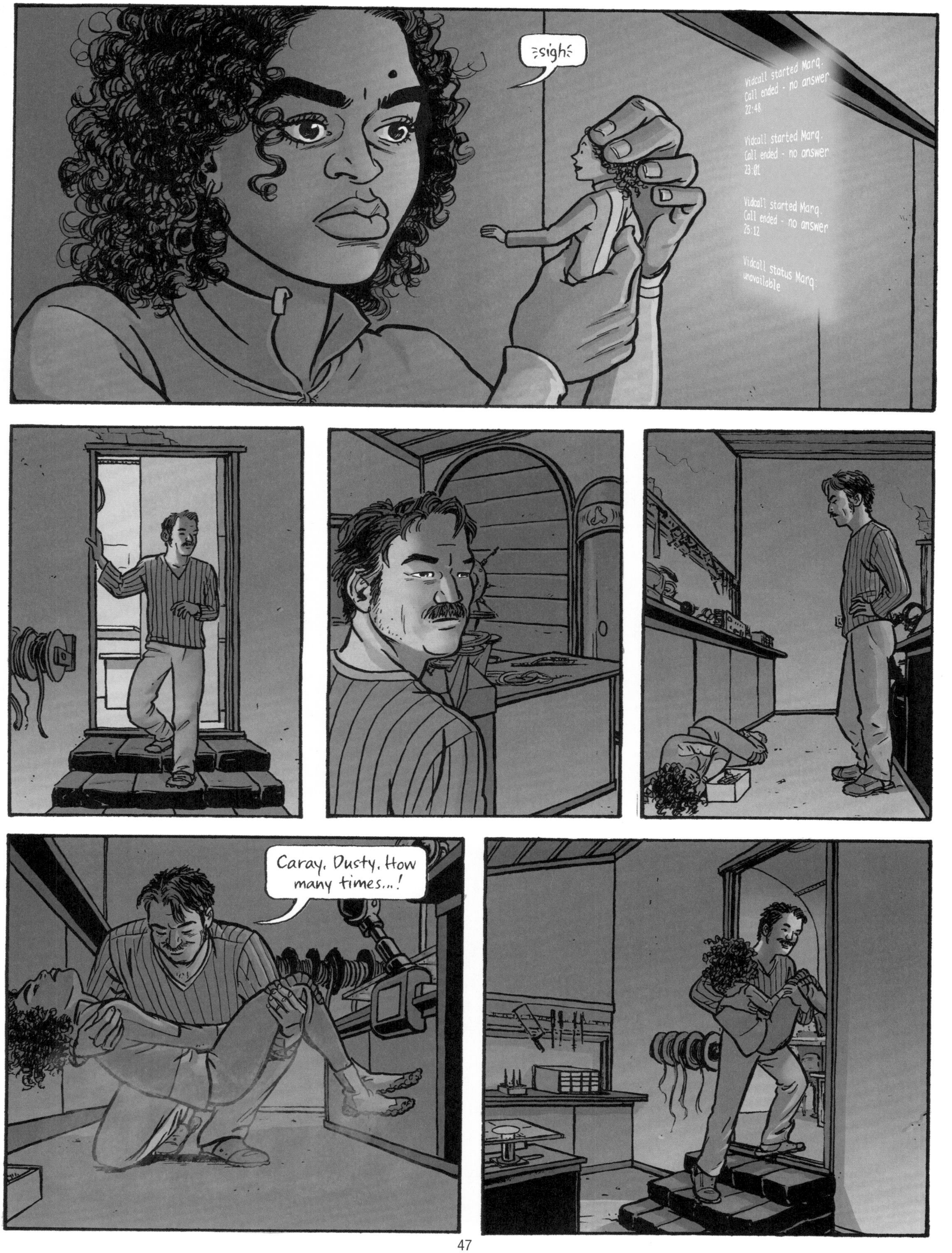
sigh
Vidcall started Marq.
Call ended - no answer
22:48
Vidcall started Marq.
Call ended - no answer
23:01
Vidcall started Marq.
Call ended - no answer
25:12
Vidcall status Marq:
unavailable
Caray, Dusty. How many times...!

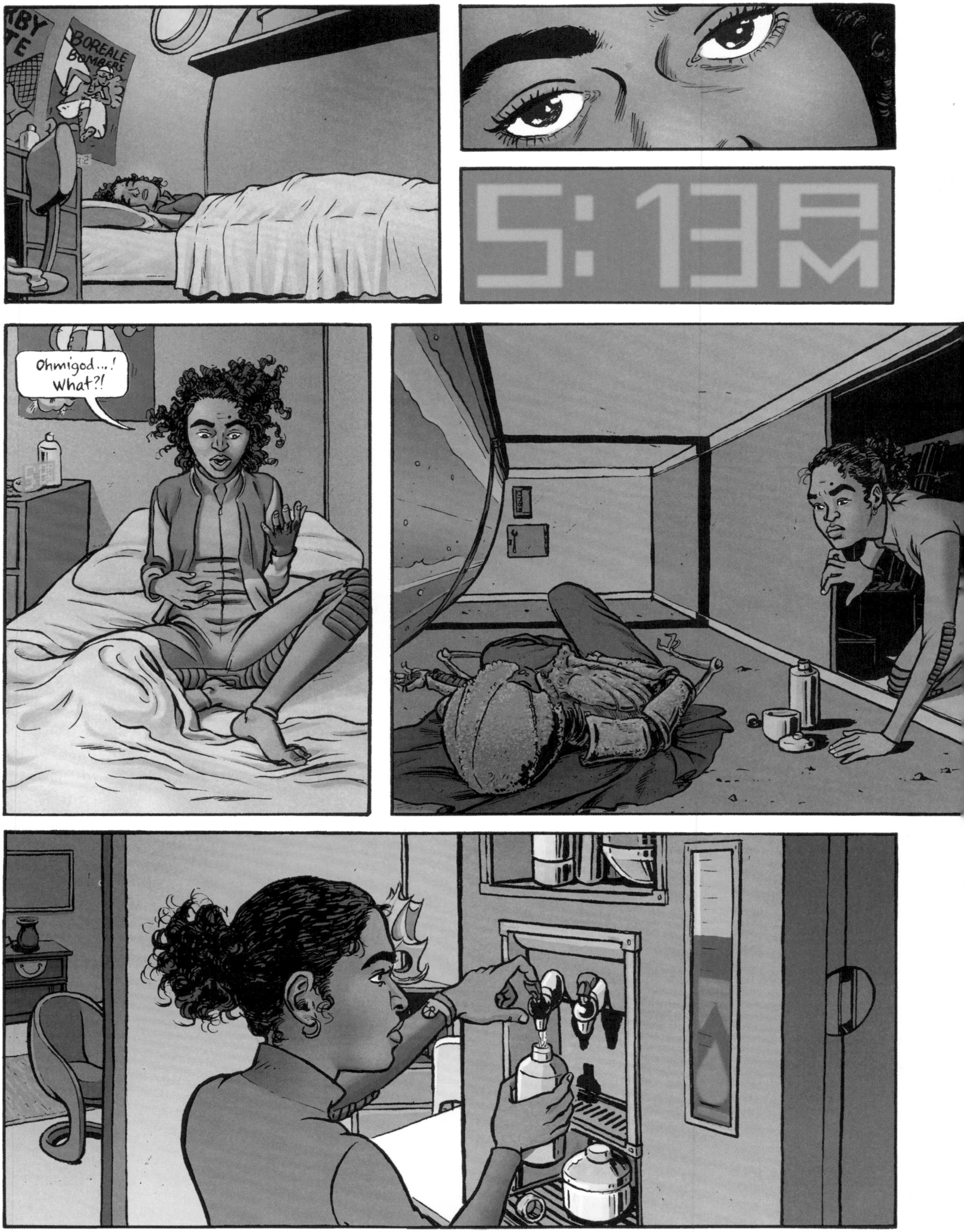
BOREALE BOMBERS
5:13 AM
Ohmigod...! What?!

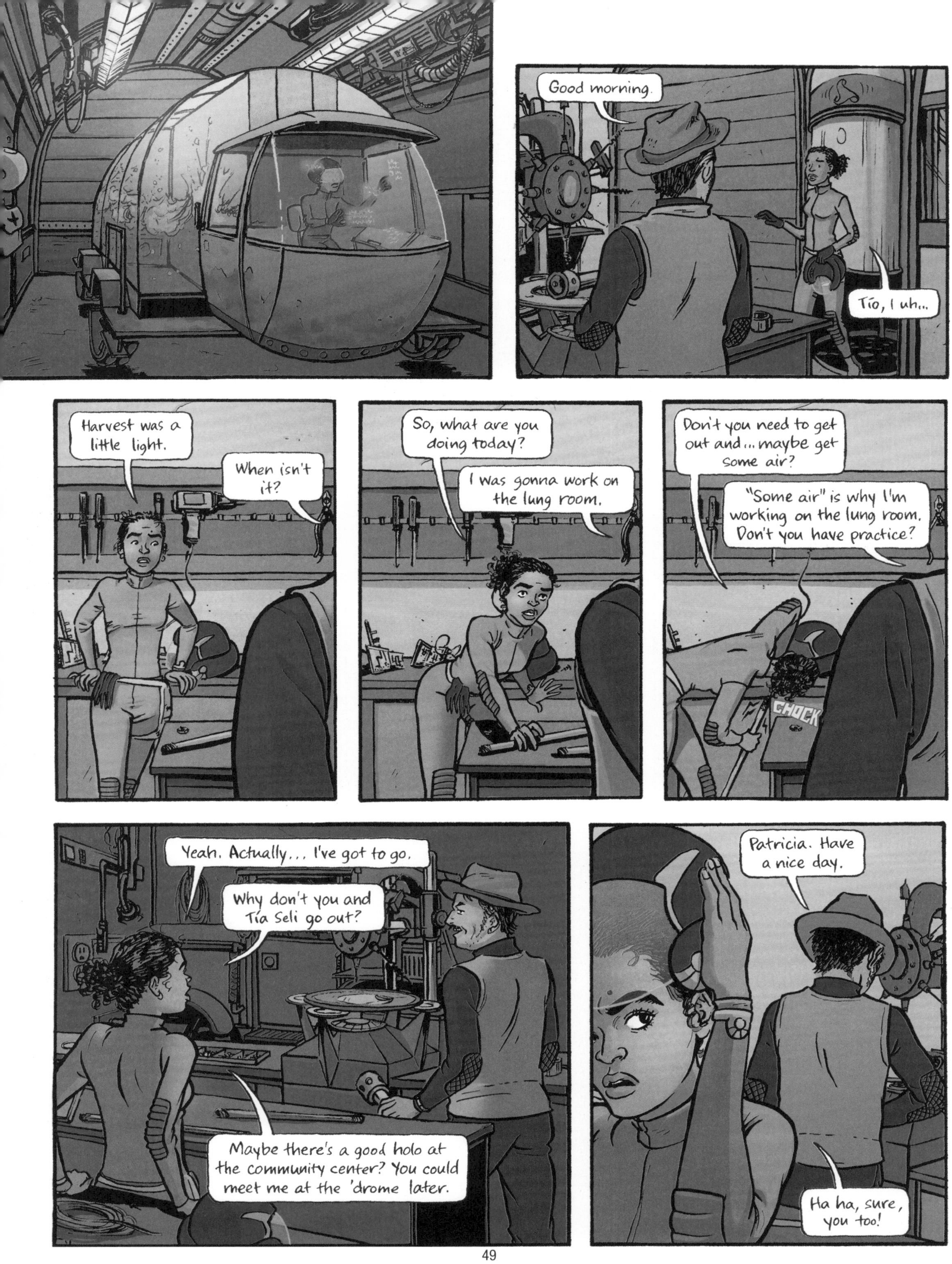

Good morning.
Tío, I uh...
Harvest was a little light.
When isn't it?
So, what are you doing today?
I was gonna work on the lung room.
Don't you need to get out and... maybe get some air?
"Some air" is why I'm working on the lung room. Don't you have practice?
CHOCK
Yeah. Actually... I've got to go.
Why don't you and Tía Seli go out?
Maybe there's a good holo at the community center? You could meet me at the 'drome later.
Patricia. Have a nice day.
Ha ha, sure, you too!

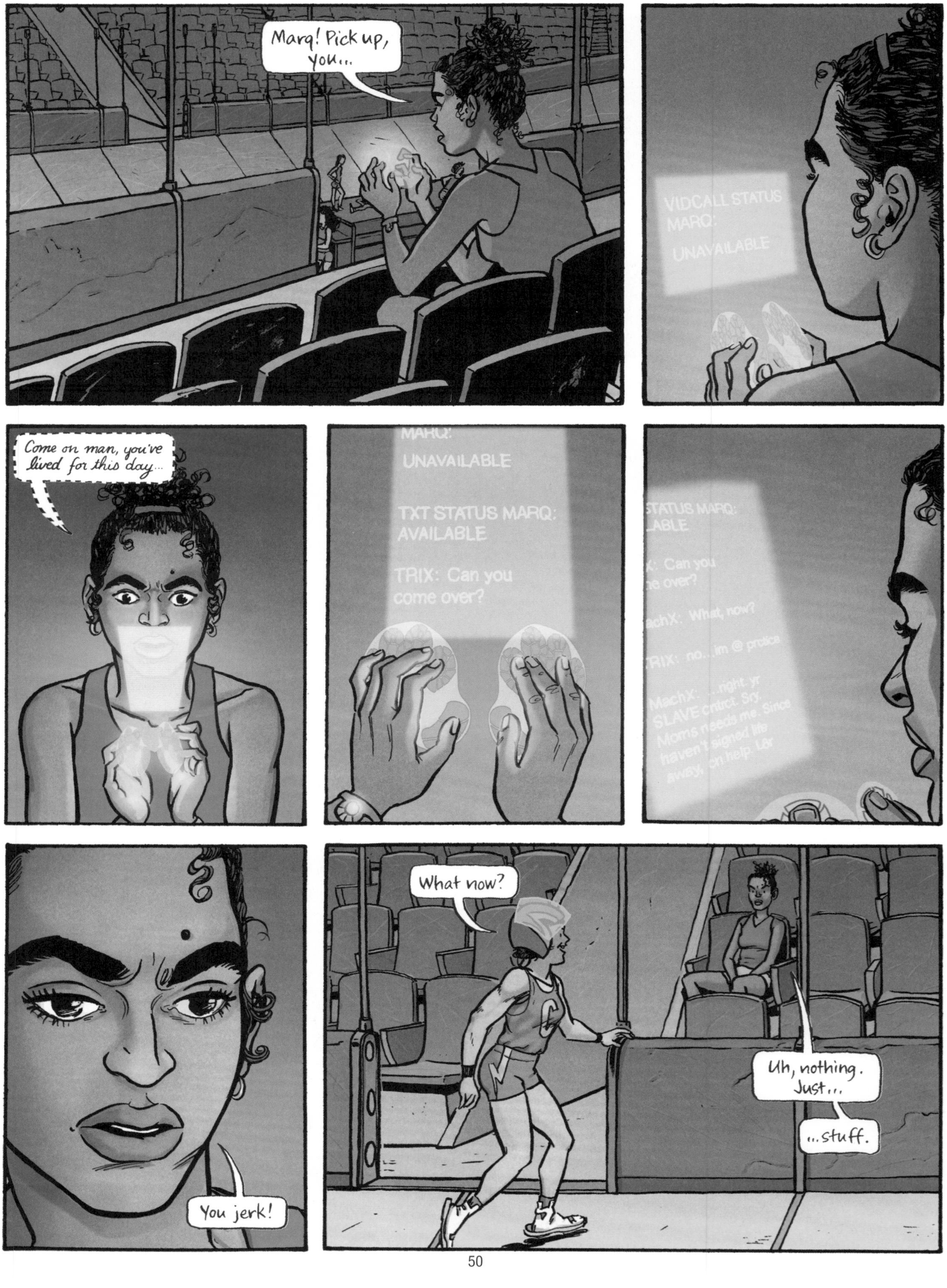
Marq! Pick up, you...
VIDCALL STATUS MARQ:
UNAVAILABLE
Come on man, you've lived for this day...
MARQ:
UNAVAILABLE
TXT STATUS MARQ: AVAILABLE
TRIX: Can you come over?
STATUS MARQ:
MachX: What, now?
TRIX: no... im @ prctice
MachX: ...night. yr SLAVE cntrct. Sry. Moms needs me. Since haven't signed life away, cn help. L8r
You jerk!
What now?
Uh, nothing. Just...
...stuff.

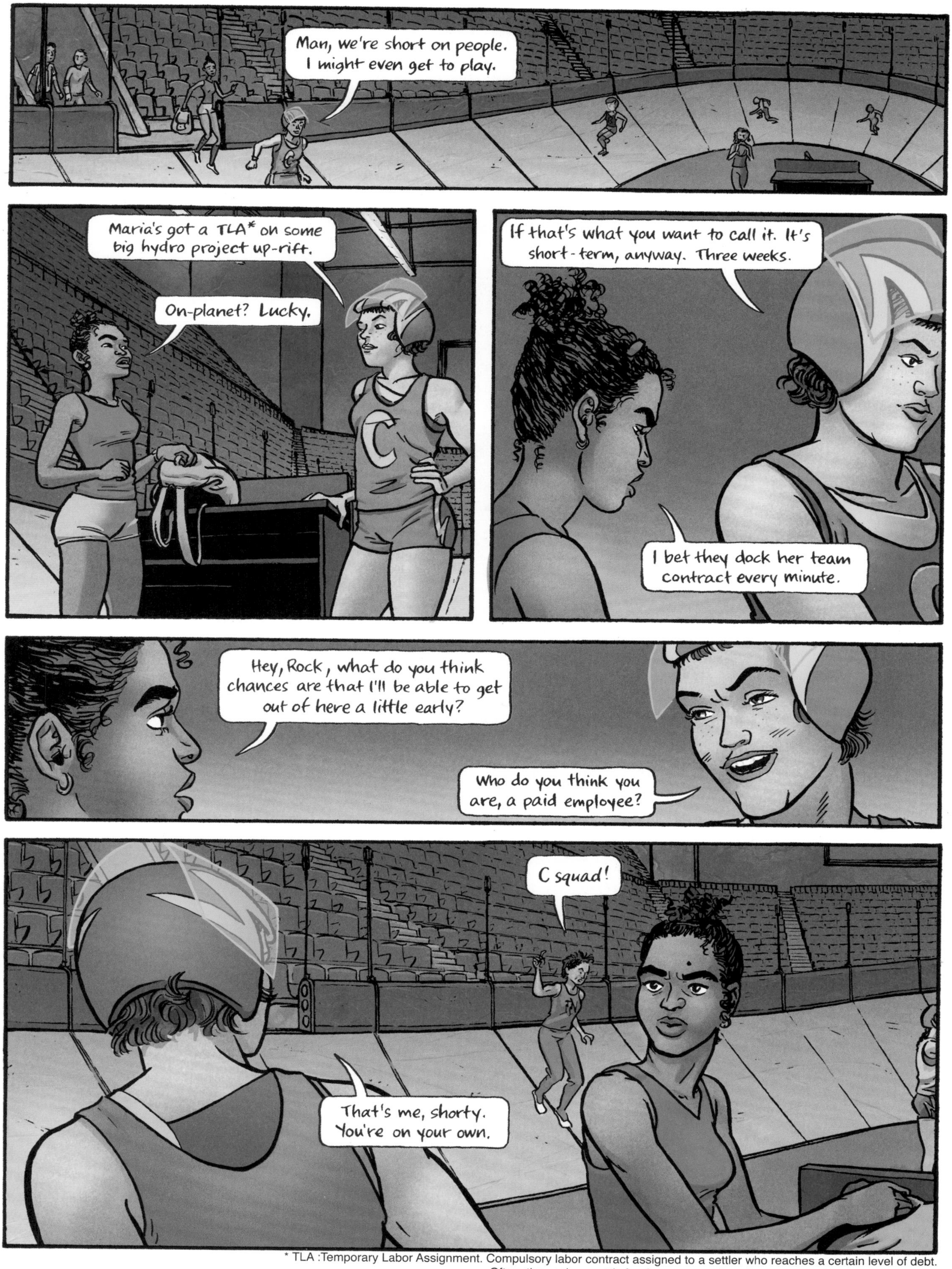
Man, we're short on people. I might even get to play.
Maria's got a TLA* on some big hydro project up-rift.
On-planet? Lucky.
If that's what you want to call it. It's short-term, anyway. Three weeks.
I bet they dock her team contract every minute.
Hey, Rock, what do you think chances are that I'll be able to get out of here a little early?
Who do you think you are, a paid employee?
C squad!
That's me, shorty. You're on your own.

* TLA :Temporary Labor Assignment. Compulsory labor contract assigned to a settler who reaches a certain level of debt. Often, the assignment is for dangerous and unpleasant asteroid mining operations.

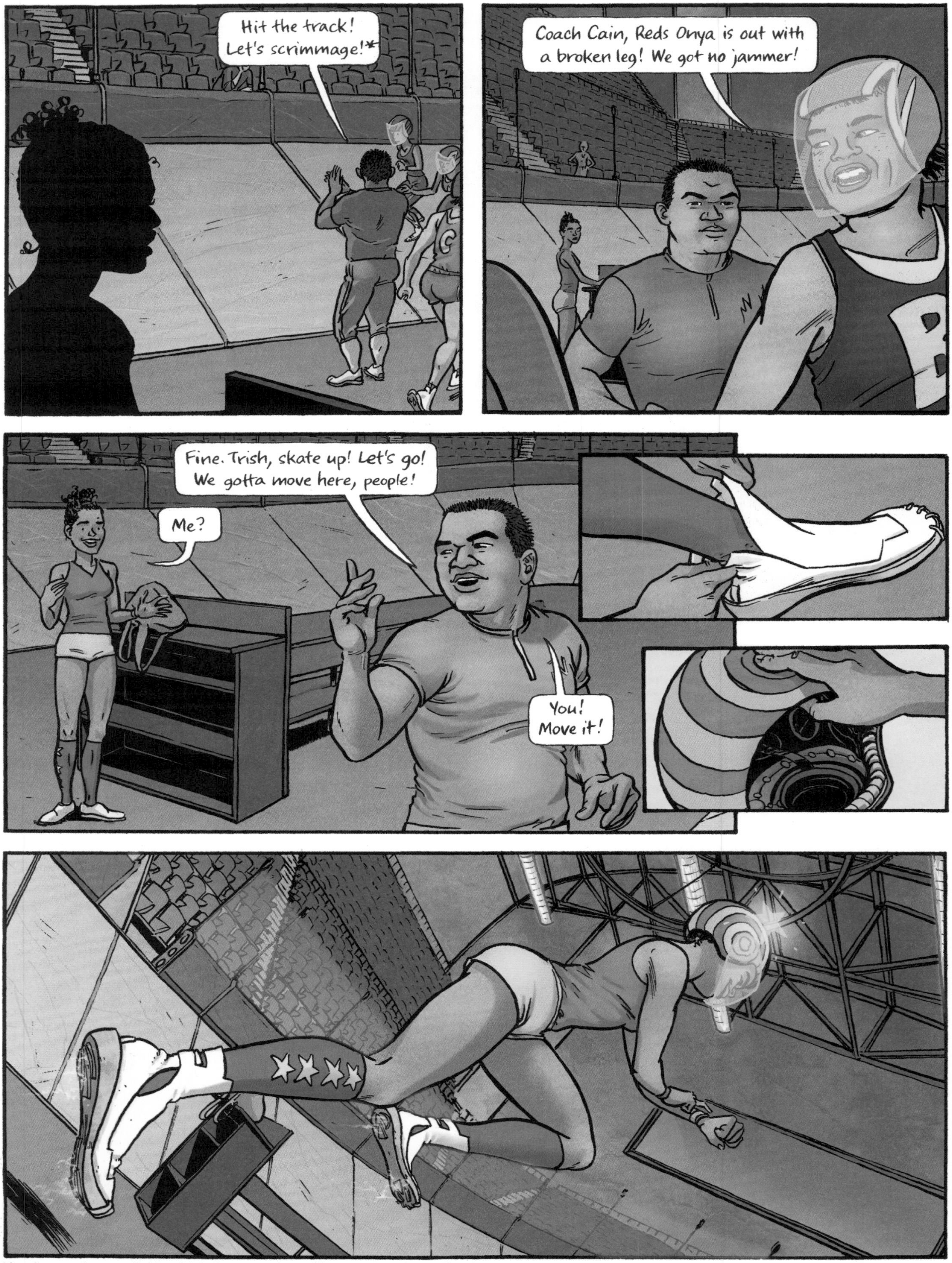
Hit the track! Let's scrimmage!*
Coach Cain, Reds Onya is out with a broken leg! We got no jammer!
Fine. Trish, skate up! Let's go! We gotta move here, people!
Me?
You! Move it!

*A scrimmage is an unofficial match between members of the same team to practice strategy.

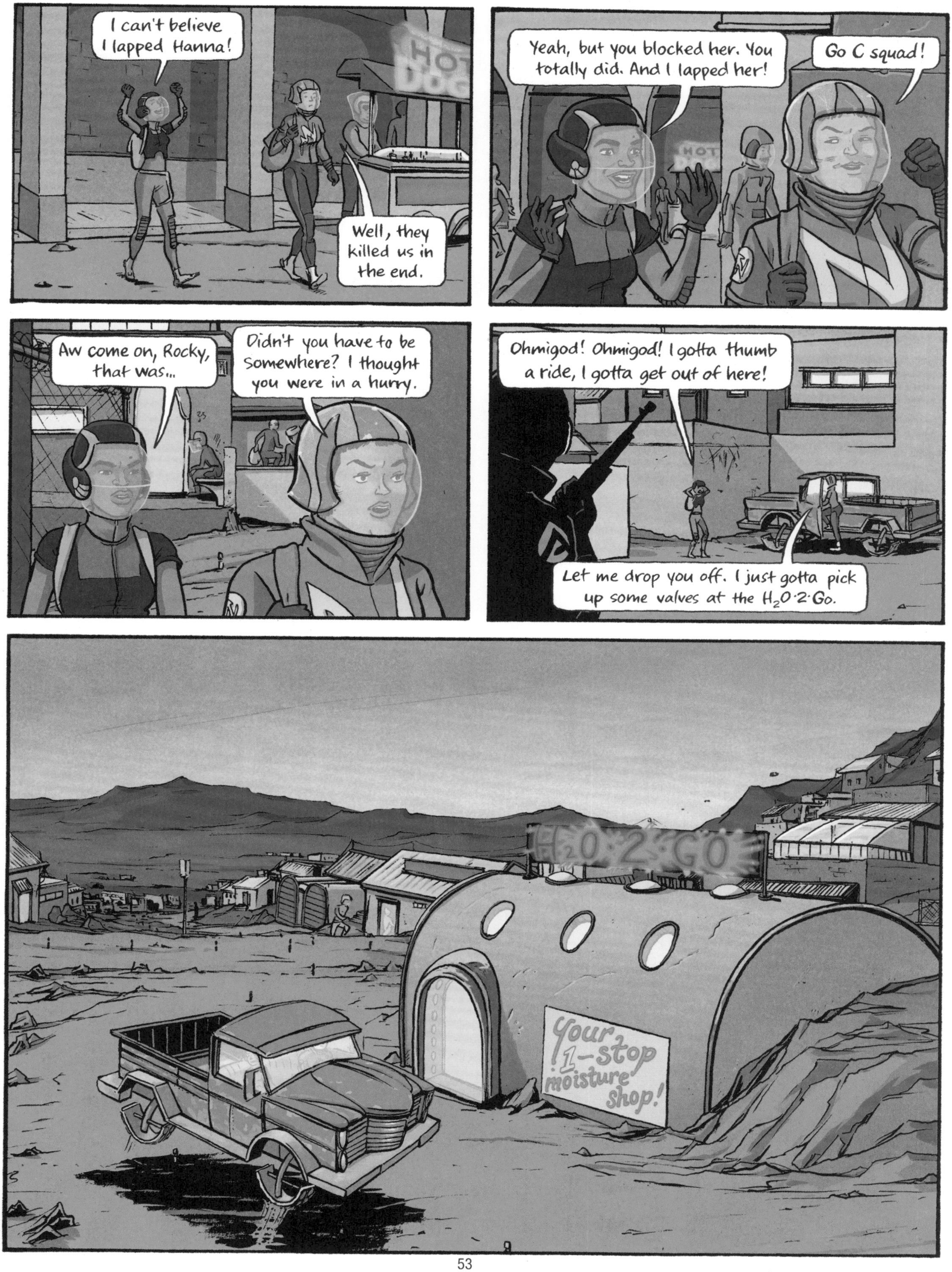
I can't believe I lapped Hanna!
Well, they killed us in the end.
Yeah, but you blocked her. You totally did. And I lapped her!
Go C squad!
Aw come on, Rocky, that was...
Didn't you have to be somewhere? I thought you were in a hurry.
Ohmigod! Ohmigod! I gotta thumb a ride, I gotta get out of here!
Let me drop you off. I just gotta pick up some valves at the H_2O·2·Go.
H_2O 2 GO
Your 1-stop moisture shop!

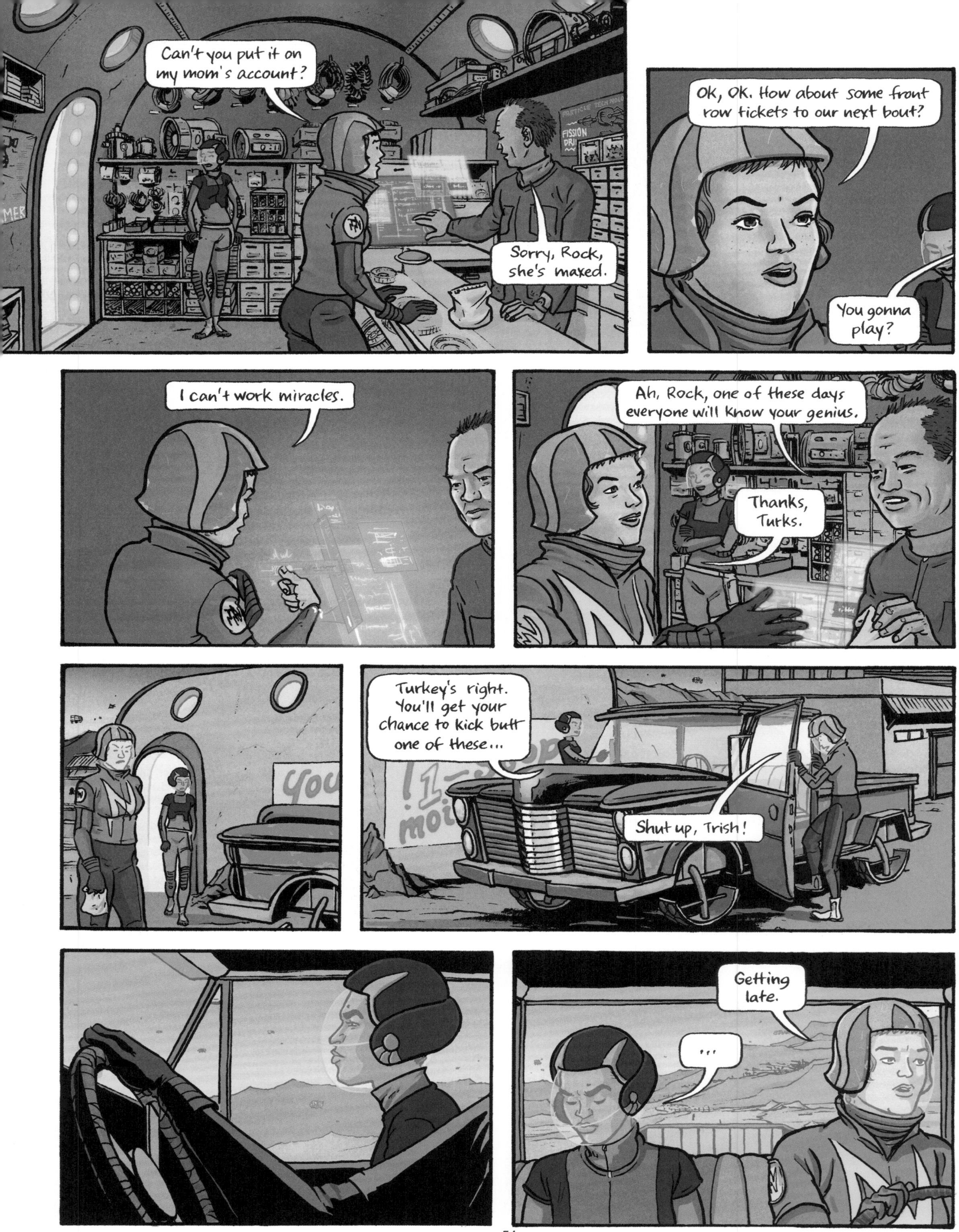
Can't you put it on my mom's account?
Sorry, Rock, she's maxed.
OK, OK. How about some front row tickets to our next bout?
You gonna play?
I can't work miracles.
Ah, Rock, one of these days everyone will know your genius.
Thanks, Turks.
Turkey's right. You'll get your chance to kick butt one of these...
Shut up, Trish!
Getting late.
...

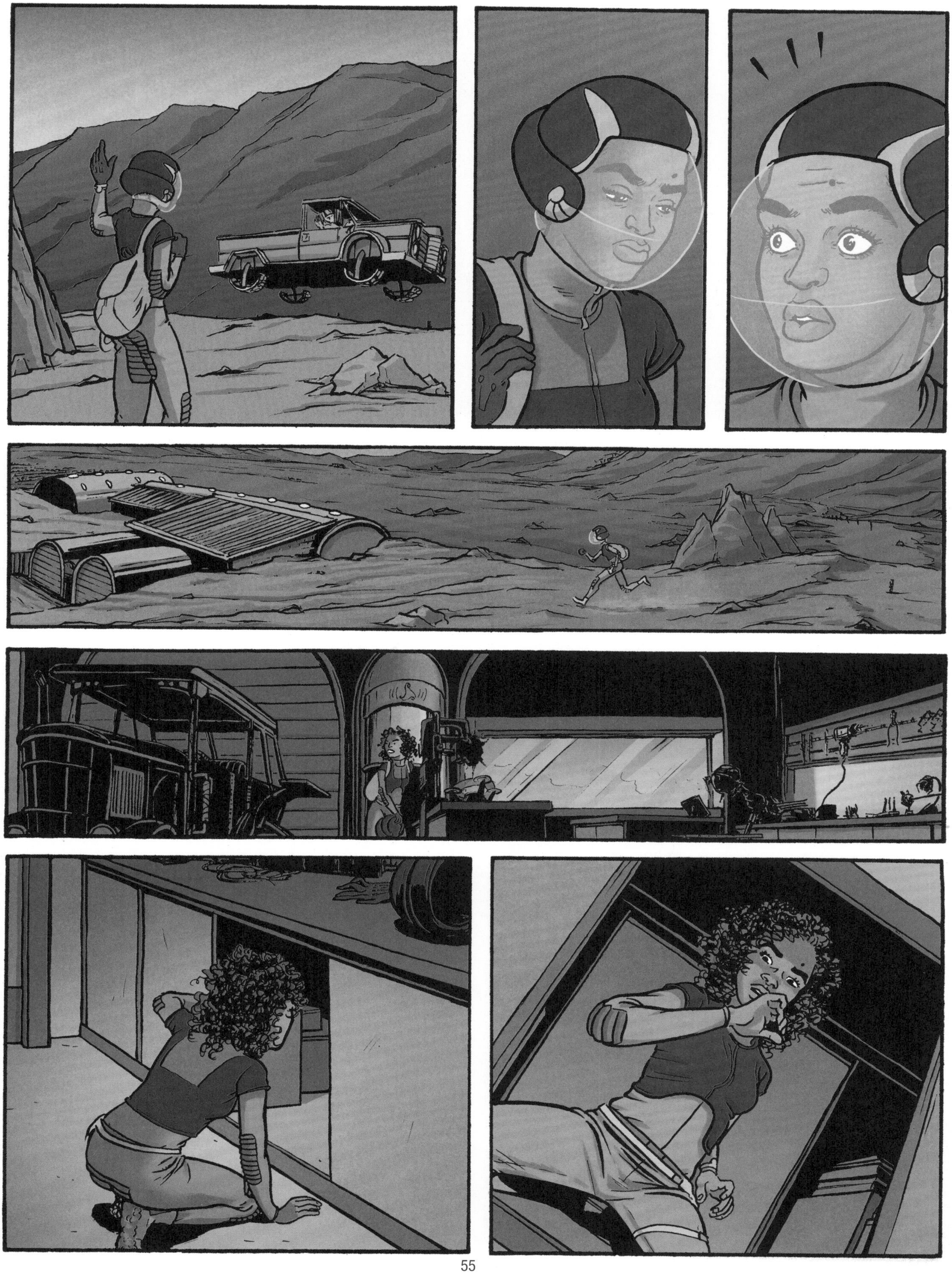

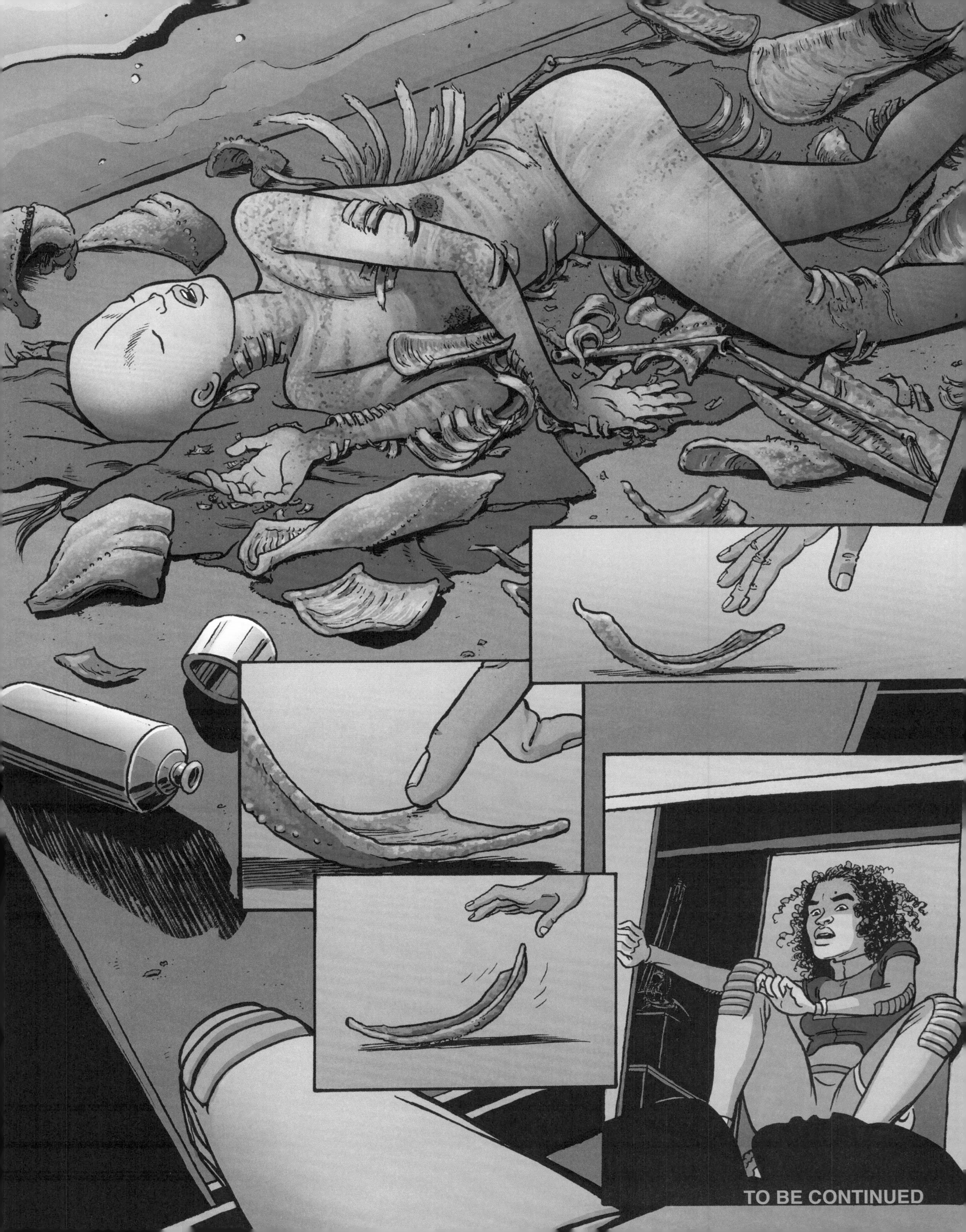
TO BE CONTINUED

Hoverderby

Hoverderby is a contact sport played by two teams of five players each, hoverskating in a counter-clockwise direction on a banked track. One player on each team is able to score points (a "jammer"), by passing players on the other team. Non-scoring players ("blockers" and "pivots") must try to assist their team's jammer while impeding the jammer of the other team.

Basics of play [edit]

This section consists of a brief overview of hoverderby rules and play. It must not be construed as a complete or definitive description of such rules. For legal and complete rules, please consult sections 11326.8890 through 12870.3345 of the Log of WBTHDA.[1]

Games, known as "bouts," consist of short "jams," periods of play of up to two minutes. A bout lasts one hour of play, divided into two half-hour periods.

Jammers, indicated by two holographic stars on either side of their helmets, line up on the start line behind pivots (with a holographic stripe on their helmets), and blockers (no indication on helmets). At the whistle, players' hover skates are released from the track, and they must begin forward motion or they will slide into the infield, earning a penalty.

Jammers must complete a full non-scoring pass of all opposing players before they may begin scoring points. The first jammer to pass all opposing players is named the "lead jammer" and acquires a third holographic star above her helmet. The lead jammer has the ability to end the jam at any time by patting her hips with both hands. The pivot and the other blockers, may attempt to block any player on the opposing team using any legal blocking zone, and may contact any legal target zone. These zones consist of, essentially, the torso, hips, and upper arms (see section 12129.1120 of the Log for specifics). Hits and contact in other areas are penalties.

A team may field a roster of up to 14 players per game, five of whom will play in any one jam.

Required safety gear includes helmets with four-quadrant forcefields installed, and derbydromes must be equipped with forcefield barriers to protect audiences from players, who may be moving at up to 75 kph.

[1] Women's Banked Track Hoverderby Association

History [edit]

Hoverderby has its roots in the 20th century, in two distinct phases. The first of these sprang out of endurance roller skating races. In the mid 1930s, under the direction of sports promoter Leo Seltzer, What was then known as "Roller Derby" morphed into a professional contact sport played between two teams of five players each, on a banked track.

DERBY GEAR: THEN AND NOW

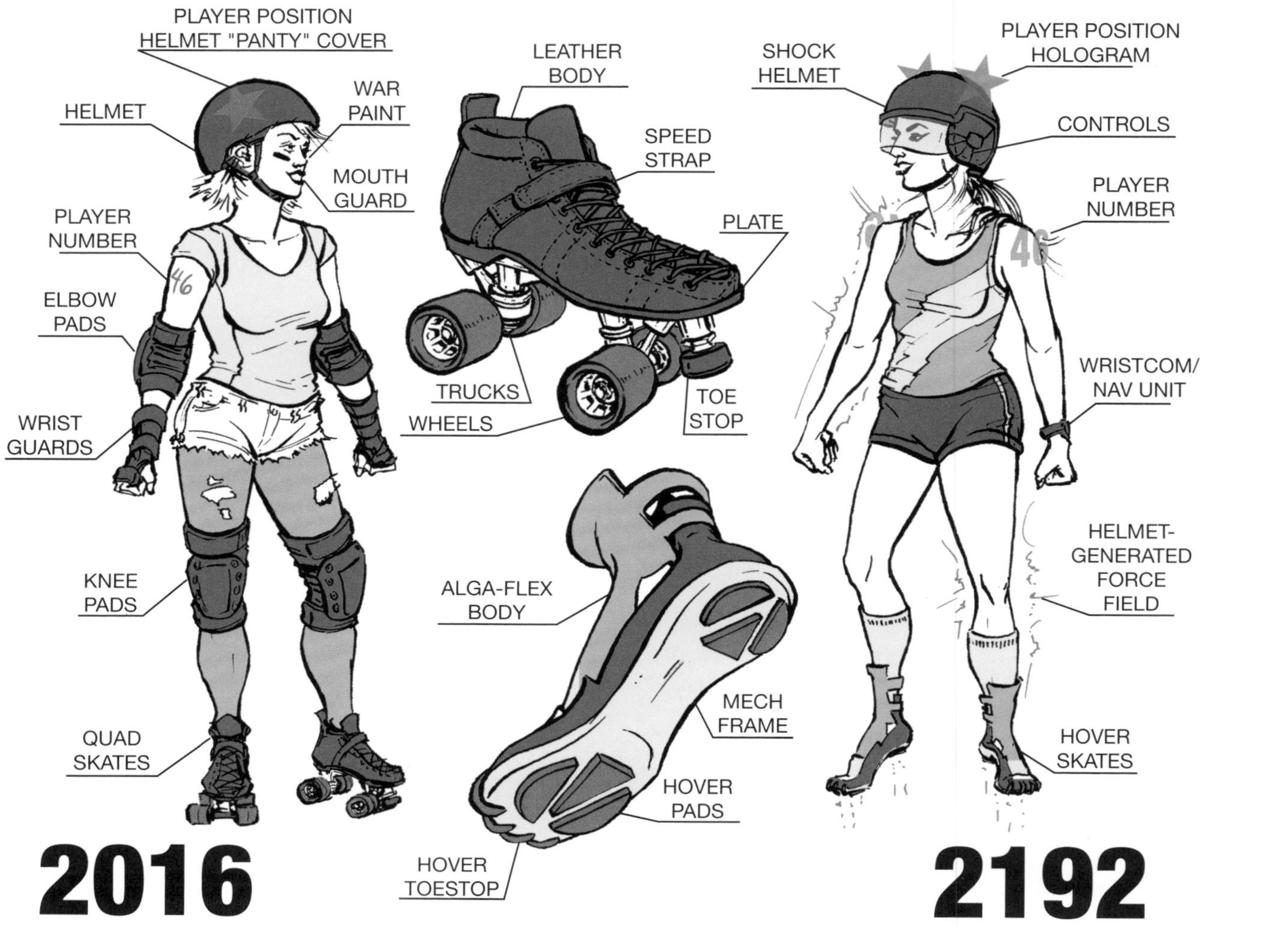
PLAYER POSITION HELMET "PANTY" COVER
HELMET
WAR PAINT
MOUTH GUARD
PLAYER NUMBER
ELBOW PADS
WRIST GUARDS
KNEE PADS
QUAD SKATES
2016
LEATHER BODY
SPEED STRAP
PLATE
TRUCKS
WHEELS
TOE STOP
ALGA-FLEX BODY
MECH FRAME
HOVER PADS
HOVER TOESTOP
SHOCK HELMET
PLAYER POSITION HOLOGRAM
CONTROLS
PLAYER NUMBER
WRISTCOM/ NAV UNIT
HELMET-GENERATED FORCE FIELD
HOVER SKATES
2192

Back matter art and colors by Lydia Roberts

Photo Credit: L. Roberts

At that time, skaters wore “quad roller skates,” boots with four wheels attached in a rectangular configuration, as hover tech was not developed until 2078.

This phase of development saw some of the basic rules of the sport develop, but it was also marked by exploitative violence and fictional storylines akin to what spectators would have expected from professional wrestling at the time (this is well before the lo-EarthOrbit FullContact BattleSphere was developed). This iteration of the sport was designed to appeal to spectators of television, the two-dimensional video medium prevalent at the time.

This early era of derby was over by the end of that century. In 2002, however, the sport was unexpectedly revived by a group of women in Austin, Texas, who founded an all-female amateur league. (At that time, Texas, a region of the southwest part of the then-United States, still had a livable climate. See entry on pre-desertification southwest North America/major cities.) Though it was played on quad roller skates, and usually on a flat track, this version of derby is the true predecessor of today’s hoverderby. The rules teams play by today were developed and refined in the first few decades of the 21st century. By 2014, there were over 1200 amateur leagues, most of them exclusively female, playing all around the world. Male and co-ed teams began picking up steam as well, and by 2050, it was unusual to find any medium-sized town almost anywhere in the world without its own amateur league. As the world approached the Meltdown, derby proved to be a durable and attractive pastime for a humanity on the brink.

When hovertech was commercialized in 2073-2078, one of the first applications was to derby. Immediately, however, it became clear that the canonical flat-track and flat-track rules would not work for hoverskating. The gory impalement and death of Avocado Pitts of the Manitoba Mamas as she skidded off the flat track during the Playoffs of 2078 on the vidblast in every fan's living room was the tipping point for the world, already reeling from billions suffering and dying from the Meltdown's floods and droughts that year. The outcry led the WFTDA (Women's Flat Track Derby Association) management to a long and very public soul searching, from which they emerged as the WBTHDA.

Banked tracks were built wherever hoverskates were in use, to contain the enormous speed and inertia of the radical (at the time) new technology. Nonetheless, the 2080s and 2090s saw many serious injuries. As soon as forcefields became commonly available, they were mandated in all hoverderbydromes in barrier walls, and in 2114, by the time virtually all derby was hoverderby, personal forcefields were required in all derby helmets.

Avocado Pitts   Photo Credit: L. Roberts

The steeply-banked track of today's derby necessitates speedy play and allows for dramatic action, and it's widely thought that these developments have contributed to the enormous popularity of derby, which has held its position as humanity's number one sport for the last 38 years.

Hoverderby on Mars   [edit]

Derby was exported to Mars with the Pioneers. It's well known that Mars' first settlers were derby fans, but they also improvised a flat track in the midst of their first rough scientific settlement, at Robinson Crater. Unfortunately, it soon became apparent that the dust kicked up by all that skating and falling would gum up every hoverpad and intake in the vicinity, so they abandoned the recreation league within three months.

2016 Conferences

1 Arcadia conference, based in the Vastitas Borealis, home of Mars's number one team, the Boreale Bombers.

2 Southern conference, based in Hellas.

3 Utopia conference, based in Utopia planitia.

4 Marineris conference (AKA the Duster league) based in the Marineris Chasma.

Full list of Martian WBTHDA teams

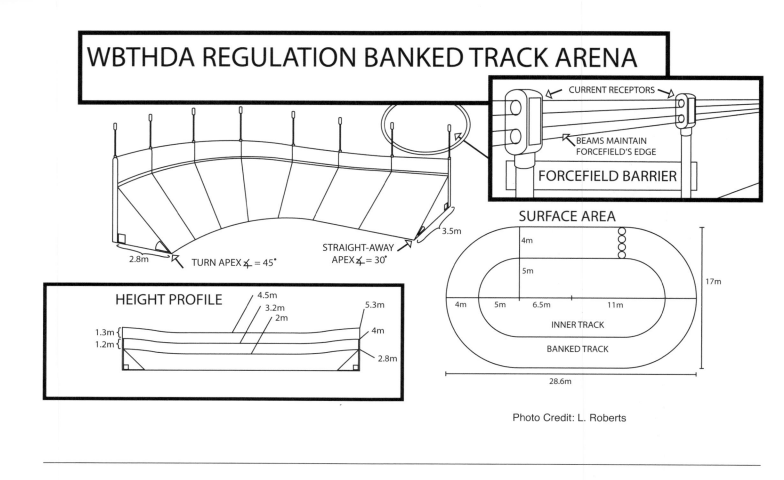

WBTHDA REGULATION BANKED TRACK ARENA

CURRENT RECEPTORS

BEAMS MAINTAIN
FORCEFIELD'S EDGE

FORCEFIELD BARRIER

TURN APEX ∡ = 45°

STRAIGHT-AWAY
APEX ∡ = 30°

2.8m

3.5m

HEIGHT PROFILE

4.5m
3.2m
2m
5.3m
1.3m
1.2m
4m
2.8m

SURFACE AREA

4m
5m
4m
5m
6.5m
11m
17m

INNER TRACK

BANKED TRACK

28.6m

Photo Credit: L. Roberts

Third wave settlers build the first crude derbydrome in Zubrinsville. Amateur teams played in this drome for 25 years, before it fell into disrepair. Today it can be visited as the Museum of Derby and Hoversport on Mars.

Derby became a professional sport on Mars in 2128 (39ME[1]), and there are today four conferences of teams.

[1] Mars Era year 39, which spans 2128-2129 CE

Radsuits

The sleek and powerful radsuit of today is evolved from bulky compression suits of the first Mars Pioneers. The Martian atmosphere at the time of the Pioneers' arrival was extremely thin, and average ambient outdoor temperature was –55°C, lower during the frequent dust storms. Habitats and work modules were pressurized and built under the surface, and any surface walks required pressure suits and oxygen supplies.

As terraforming efforts took hold in the beginning of the 22nd century, gradually various features of the pressure suits were rendered unnecessary, and the modern radsuit evolved. In 2113 (31ME),

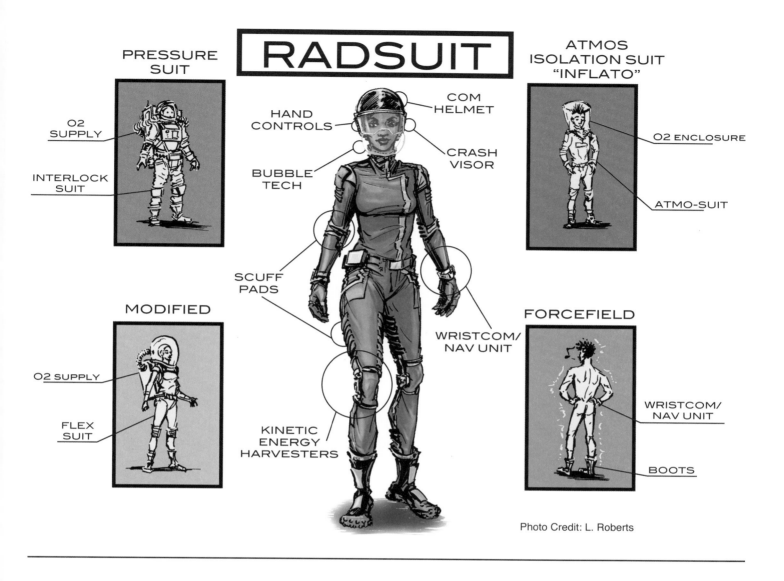

RADSUIT

PRESSURE SUIT

- O2 SUPPLY
- INTERLOCK SUIT

MODIFIED

- O2 SUPPLY
- FLEX SUIT

HAND CONTROLS

BUBBLE TECH

SCUFF PADS

KINETIC ENERGY HARVESTERS

COM HELMET

CRASH VISOR

WRISTCOM/ NAV UNIT

ATMOS ISOLATION SUIT "INFLATO"

- O2 ENCLOSURE
- ATMO-SUIT

FORCEFIELD

- WRISTCOM/ NAV UNIT
- BOOTS

Photo Credit: L. Roberts

atmospheric pressure was deemed sufficient for comfortable non-pressurized surface walks. By 2138 (44ME), global temperatures had stabilized to the point that there is rarely life-threatening cold weather (except during dust storms). Atmospheric concentration of CO_2 remains poisonous to humans, and O_2 levels too low to breathe without supplementation and/or filtration, but masks to do this job are small and lightweight, and under normal circumstances, supplemental O_2 is not required. Kinetic energy pumps power the HUD, gas exchange, water conservation, and temperature controls of a modern radsuit.

Of course, cosmic radiation remains a threat, but radiation shielding was crude in those early suits, contributing to high levels of DNA damage and disease. Terraformation researchers continue to work on methods to create the magnetosphere that Mars still lacks, and drug treatments for radiation exposure are very effective. Nonetheless, one of the most important functions of a radsuit is the shielding it offers the wearer. This shielding is also required to be installed in all buildings.

Despite the obvious utility of radiation shielding, the Planetary Council of Mars has felt it necessary to issue a series of regulations in the last few years having to do with radsuits. Many Mars citizens have taken to wearing Atmos Isolation Suits (popularly known as "inflatos"), partial radsuits, and even flimsy rebreathers with goggles, all of which will assist with making the atmosphere breathable, but will not protect the wearer from radiation. Wearing nothing but a forcefield is quite dangerous and has produced outraged Pundits on the vidblast, but regulation has not yet been issued regarding this fashion among the young and trendy.

Arex has issued rules for those with an ACSOD[1] of –20K per individual (in other words, an individual eligible for a TLA[2]), requiring full radsuit use at all times for the protection of Arex's investment and the individual's family ACSOD. Violators may be prosecuted.

[1] Ares Collective Statement of Debt

[2] Temporary Labor Assignment

The Homestead Debate

By 2062, Earth was locked into a warming feedback loop, headed for the Meltdown. Tac Nontilor, the visionary founder of Arex, then known as Ares Exploration Corporation, had sent several missions to Mars already, including the Mayflower, one of nine ships now thought of as carrying the Pioneers. Rapid desertification in central Africa, Australia, and in the south of the United States of America threatened to spark a world war, as it did in fact in 2076. This was the scene when Nontilor delivered his electrifying talk at TED 2062 proposing a Homesteading effort on Mars. Nontilor suggested that

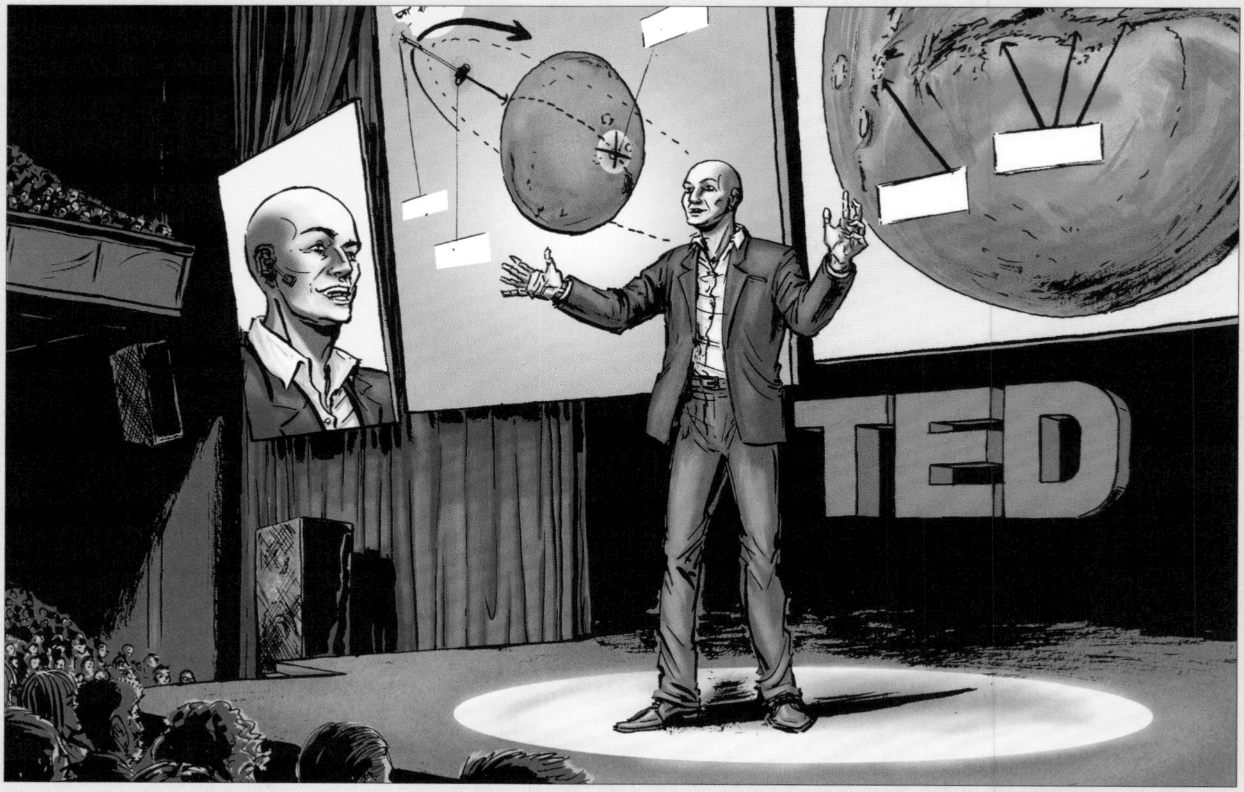
TED

Tac Nontilor at TED 2062

Photo Credit: L. Roberts

Homesteading citizens arrive on the first Arex transport 2072.

Photo Credit: L. Roberts

the United Nations (precursor to the Planetary Council of Mars) offer land to colonists on Mars in exchange for developing that land. Arex would provide transport to Mars and materials that the colonists would need to begin life there (habitats, farm equipment, pressure suits, even food and water), in exchange for a percentage of their products, or their labor for a certain proportion of their time on Arex development projects. Nontilor's proposal was akin to a National Guard contract, and was proposed in a spirit of helping those whose lives were coming apart due to the environment's collapse. Nonetheless, it was immediately attacked by pundits as a kind of "slavery," which argument was completely undermined by the voluntary nature of the contracts.

The UN, unable to muster sufficient troops to control the unrest in the most severely affected areas of Earth, immediately embraced the idea, which then provided a much-needed safety valve that postponed the worst violence until the war in 2076-2081. No colonist was forced to emigrate, and in fact, despite the dangers and unknowns, demand was immediately very high. Arex's shuttles began delivering indentured settlers to Mars in 2072 (11ME), and, as the space elevators on Mars and Earth were completed, continued on an increasingly rapid schedule for the next 15 years, peaking in 2087.

Criticism in the media by Terrans opposed to the program changed in character over time from accusations of a new style of slavery to the accusation that Arex could take more people to Mars if it tried. Conditions on Earth deteriorated and attacks on the shuttles, particularly from the increasingly lawless Habitats [1], increased until the last shuttle arrived in 2110 (30ME).

A total of nearly one million humans were saved by the Homestead program from almost certain destruction in the Meltdown.

[1] "Piracy Aboard the Habitats: the Decline of Humanity's Life-Saving Space Stations in the aftermath of the Meltdown". Balthazar Commission Hearings, Volume XI. Habitat Archives and Research Center. March 22, 2141. Sections IV.3245.29 to IV.5678.01

Native Martians

This page makes controversial statements, and needs to cite research as justification. Please help wiki.marsred improve this article.

(disambiguation)
- *Native martians,* non-human beings evolved on Mars (indigenous Martians)
- *Native martians,* humans born on Mars (commonly known as Martys)

Main article: Human colonization of Mars

In the last 25 years, there have been numerous but as yet unconfirmed reports of sightings of humanoid [needs citation] creatures in the Martian outback. These beings, known as "Bugs", for their insect-like [needs citation] appearance, live in caves [needs citation] and prey on humans [needs citation] living in isolated areas, such as moisture farmers in the midlands.

Arex and the PCM[1] has known about native Martians since the pioneers, but has kept that knowledge from settlers in an effort to prevent terror and panic [needs citation].

Knowledgable sources report that the natives' attacks are increasing in frequency [needs citation], and humans should gird for battle [needs citation].

[1] Planetary Council of Mars

THE MARTIAN MENACE
Native martian (artist's conception)

Photo Credit: L. Roberts